THINK YOUR WAY TO THE TOP

HOW TO SUCCEED IN BUSINESS AT ANY AGE

RON OSBORNE

WITH HEATHER GOETTER

Think Your Way to the Top
How to Succeed in Business at Any Age

Softcover ISBN: 978-1-61206-290-7
Hardcover ISBN: 978-1-61206-291-4
eBook ISBN: 978-1-61206-292-1

To purchase this book at quantity discounts, contact Aloha Publishing at alohapublishing@gmail.com

Published by:

AlohaPublishing.com

Printed in the United States of America

CONTENTS

INTRODUCTION

Sitting in my backyard under my favorite tree, watching the young people from church mingle and chat, I noticed Ryan cross the yard toward me. As he approached, I greeted him and offered him the newly vacant lawn chair next to me. I could tell something was on his mind, and he wanted to talk.

After thanking me, he dove right in. "Bishop Osborne, can I ask you a question?" Without giving me a chance to answer, he continued, "I really like working at Chick-Fil-A, but I know that I need a job that can be my career now that Aubrey and I are getting married. How do I find that?"

This was not an unusual line of questioning to me. Because of where I currently am in business and life, the owner of a successful line of storage facilities, I regularly have young or not-so-young people asking me for business and career advice. Having reached this place through hard work, learning from my mistakes, being willing to try new things, taking advantage of emerging technology, and constantly asking myself the hard questions, I love taking the time to help steer others in the right direction. Using my past experiences—both successes and failures—I hope to help others learn the easy way what I have learned over the last 45 plus years of life experience.

My life started out in extreme poverty. We were poor even before my dad passed away when I was 10 years old. After that, my mom worked hard to provide for us, but we still ate mostly what we grew and hunted. My parents didn't give me any financial advantage. I had to start at the bottom and work my way out of the poverty cycle.

I started at a shoe store, learning everything I could about being a responsible employee. My next job was selling insurance. I did that, first for another company, then for myself. I soon got an opportunity to work for Blue Shield, with the potential to become the director of sales.

Even when that came to nothing, my career continued to flourish because of the choices I made and the calculated risks I took. After a few strategic decisions, including refusing to take a bonus and sign a non-compete clause, starting my own company, and reluctantly selling that company years later, I am now president and CEO of a thriving self-storage business. It is not because I am amazingly brilliant, but because I learned how to start and grow a business (or two). The learning journey wasn't always easy—sometimes I had to learn the hard way. But I learned.

Occasionally I hear from friends or neighbors about their latest business ventures. Some are solid and I can see they will do well. But occasionally I want to shake my head, sit them down, and ask them a few important questions about their plan.

I love to share the foundational business principles that led me to where I am today. They are essential to choosing a career, starting a business, growing that business, and having a business mindset. There are a few solid principles that everyone needs to know. These principles will position you on the path to success, especially if you desire to own a business. However, the same principles will help you, as an employee, move up the ladder of your chosen field into a more prosperous position.

The principles are practical but more importantly, they are about having the right mindset. So many people jump into their chosen careers focused on if they have the specific skills necessary to do their particular job. But they miss the more important skills to have: evaluation, critical thinking, humility, question asking, and the most important skill of all, the ability to do what needs to be done.

These skills are needed right from the beginning when choosing a career. They are needed when learning how to run a business, when connecting with employers, employees, or clients, and when learning how to overcome challenges. They are needed both personally and professionally.

While learning these skills, you will be gaining a business mindset. And having a business mindset will empower you to turn your aspirations into action and create the life you desire. It will challenge you to think outside the box, embrace change, and continuously strive for growth and improvement. With a business mindset, you will develop the resilience, creativity, and leadership skills necessary to overcome challenges and be successful. Most importantly, it will give you the confidence and know-how to pursue a career and turn it into a profitable and meaningful business.

Embrace the power of a business mindset and let it be the foundation for a life filled with success, fulfillment, and endless possibilities.

1

MAKE MONEY IN YOUR CAREER AND LET YOUR PASSION PROJECTS BE HOBBIES

The number one piece of advice I offer people is to choose a career wisely. So many people dream about making their hobbies into a career. They are passionate about what they do but don't take the time to ask themselves the right questions, evaluate the culture and economy, think about how the business can grow, and project what can happen in the future (both good and bad). Some of these answers take research, critical thinking, and listening to wise counsel.

Walking into a career with your eyes wide open and knowing as much as possible about all possible outcomes is essential for success.

People also don't consider the fact that doing their hobby full time can turn something they love into a job that no longer brings them joy. The day-in-and-day-out work of building a business can take away the creative passion of whatever they love about their hobby.

A few years ago, my neighbors came over to visit. I had not seen him or his wife for quite a while, and the conversation naturally shifted to what they were doing.

"It's been really tough lately. Our store is not doing well, and we might need to close it if things don't turn around." I asked them what type of store it was. They told me that it was a women's boutique. They talked about how they needed to sell a certain dollar amount each day, and not only were they not reaching it, but they realized too late that the store was not in a highly visible area, so all the stores around them were suffering.

After they left, I shook my head in frustration. They had not done their research, and now they had to start over financially even though they were in their 50s.

Young people are particularly prone to making the mistake of trying to turn their hobbies into their careers. The current "wisdom" that is out there says to *follow your passion.* But I have found that passion often doesn't lead you anywhere. Yes, there are the one-in-a-million stories of someone's passion creating a mega-empire, but that is like playing the lottery. There is an extremely high probability of failure.

So many young people want to be video game testers, social media influencers, digital artists, photographers, and the like.

And yes, it is possible to create a business or career from those things, but it is not probable.

For me, the dream would have been to be a professional golfer. I love golf but was realistic enough to know I could never have made it. I was content to enjoy it as my hobby.

Picking a career that can grow, make good money consistently, maintain long-term sustainability, and pivot as the economy and technology change will ensure success. It's also important to understand marketing, cash flow, technology, and customers to keep you on the road to financial security.

Knowing yourself—your strengths and weaknesses—is imperative. Are you good with people? Do you solve problems well? How are your technical skills? Are you good with a computer? Can you be self-motivated? What are your physical limitations? Evaluating and being honest with yourself will help you make the right choice in your career.

On the other hand, don't underestimate your ability to educate yourself, grow in business, and learn from your mistakes. Having the right skills and mindset in business is essential.

The Right Mindset for Business Changes Everything

You are ahead of the game when you have the right mindset for business. Understanding that a career is long-term helps you choose wisely. Some jobs have unlimited potential and growth, while others have a ceiling, stopping your growth potential, no matter how talented you are or how long and hard you have worked. Some jobs require you to be physically fit and don't work well for people with physical challenges or could have limitations as you age. Some jobs make good money but don't pay anything when you're not working. And there are more ideal jobs that can provide both semi-passive and residual income.

Knowing how much a career will cost in terms of money, time, or other types of investment is important. Some jobs, like working at McDonald's, for example, require very little initial investment and start with low pay and low responsibilities, but they also offer the ability to move up the ladder. Some people choose to work at McDonald's or other top franchises because of the reliable pay, teamwork environment, and long-term benefits.

In many professional fields, like healthcare, technology, and even insurance, there are many opportunities to learn on the job and earn excellent pay without much up-front investment. Many companies will train you from the ground up. Others will even pay for degrees and certifications in areas of specialty. (More about this in chapter 2.)

Other jobs require money and time commitment, and it's important to factor these costs into the job's long-term potential to determine whether it will meet your needs. For example, to become a Medical Assistant (MA) in the medical field costs about $15,000 and nine months of full-time schooling. For that money and time investment, the average MA salary is about $35,000 per year. The salary caps out around $45,000, so if you need to make more than that in the future, it would be a good idea to look into another career that has a higher earning potential.

A solid job choice in professional trades is often overlooked because of the time and cost commitment. A good example of this would be becoming an electrical lineman. The schooling costs about $17,000 and takes 15 weeks. The average base salary of a lineman is about $38,000 but with experience, can grow to over $100,000. However, to be a lineman, you need to be physically fit and willing to work outside year-round. It could be a great career for a couple of decades, allowing you to wisely invest in real estate and grow the skills to own a business later in your life when you're no longer physically capable of the job.

Our society needs all sorts of people to fill all kinds of jobs. We need high-achieving, organized, type-A people to lead large corporations, and we need the relaxed, love-to-be-outdoors people to hold flags for traffic during road construction. Having the right mindset and understanding the benefits and limitations of your professional choices will help you find the right job and career.

Successful People Consider Timing, Technology, Training, and Talent When Starting or Pivoting in Business

Consider the four Ts of success: timing, technology, training, and talent. These four areas determine, 90 percent of the time, whether you will be successful in a career. Carefully evaluating each of these Ts will help you understand your career choices.

I talked a bit about **timing** in my first book, *The Right Kind of Rich.* In that book, I used the example of Blockbuster, the video store. If someone had opened a Blockbuster store in 1998, they would have joined this franchise at the height of their success. However, they would have had to shut their doors within six years. How could they have known, you ask?

They would have had to observe the trends in the culture and technology and make an educated guess.

Technology is a tricky thing to predict unless you already have a career in that field. So much of it depends on trends, culture, and even the changes during the COVID pandemic. But taking the time to understand what you are interested in, thinking hard about how it could change in the future, and talking to intelligent, educated people—with experience in technology as well as the field you're considering—will save you from starting a career in an area that may be obsolete in just a few years.

Many manufacturing and assembly line jobs have been impacted by technology. Automation and robotics have replaced many tasks people were trained for, leading to fewer jobs in these fields. Factories now use robotic arms to assemble products and machines that can sort and package items with higher speed and precision than humans. This has led to a reduction in the number of jobs available for assembly line workers.

Retail and customer service jobs have also been affected by technology. The rise of online shopping has led to a decrease in the number of in-store jobs available. Many customers now prefer to purchase items online and have them delivered to their homes rather than going to a physical store. Additionally, virtual customer service options, such as chatbots and AI-powered customer service representatives, have replaced some human customer service jobs.

Data entry and administrative jobs have been transformed by software and automation tools which have reduced the need for humans, leading to fewer jobs available in this field. For example, optical character recognition (OCR) technology can scan documents and automatically input data into a computer system, reducing the need for workers to read the document and enter it manually.

The banking and finance industries have been technologically reshaped. Online banking and mobile apps have made many in-person transactions obsolete. Customers can now check their account balances, deposit checks, transfer money, and pay bills online or with an app, without ever having to visit a physical bank branch. Mobile apps and online trading platforms have allowed customers to invest in stocks and other financial products without needing a human financial adviser.

Finally, transportation and logistics jobs have been influenced by technology in recent years, with more change coming very soon. Taxi drivers have also suffered, losing fares because of the technology that created Uber and Lyft. And now, self-driving cars and drones have only just begun to automate the ride-sharing and delivery process. Currently, there is still a huge need for ride-sharing services in cities. There is also still a high demand for delivery drivers because of online stores, but this will decrease as drones and self-driving cars increase.

As technology continues to progress, the impact on different careers will continue to grow.

Training is another vital thing to take into consideration. People who go into professional services that require a high level of education, like doctors or dentists, have a tremendous amount of debt but usually make enough annually to pay it off quickly. However, some careers hardly ever break even.

A good example is teachers. Mathematically, that one blows my mind. It just doesn't make sense. Most teachers have to have at least a bachelor's degree as well as a teaching certificate. And then they pour their hearts and souls into teaching for very little money. If I could change that, I would, because teachers are the most influential people in a child's life besides their parents.

You need to look at the math when evaluating your career choice. You may want to be a lawyer, doctor, or highly skilled professional, but you must do the math. What's the typical income level? How long am I going to be paying off my college debt? Will a four-year degree work, or do I need a master's degree or Ph.D.?

Talent is the final area that you need to think about. I talked about this a bit in the last section. Know yourself. Understand your abilities, strengths, and weaknesses. We all work differently and have different ideal work conditions, motivations, and support needs.

Take Suzie for example. Suzie loves to be around people. She got a degree in business, not because she loved business, but because it was a solid degree that would allow her freedom to pick a career. However, she does not want a job sitting behind a desk running numbers all day. Being around people and helping them be successful brings her the most satisfaction and joy.

Not everyone is like Suzie. Some people work best behind a closed door because they love to crunch numbers, find solutions to problems, and help a business grow without interruptions in their day.

Thankfully, there are quite a few programs and tests that will help you know what your strengths and weaknesses are. The last thing you want to do is pour four to eight years of schooling into a career you end up not being good at, don't like, or have no desire to continue.

Finding the Right Career for You

One way to find a good career for yourself is to take a career assessment test. These tests help you understand your strengths, interests, and values and how they align with different careers. For example, the Myers-Briggs Type Indicator is a personality test that can help you understand your personality type and what careers may be a good fit for you. Clifton Strengths (formerly Strength Finders) is another test that identifies your top strengths. Similarly, the Strong Interest Inventory (SII) is a career assessment test that identifies your interests and how they fit well with different careers. These tests can be helpful as a starting point and provide valuable insights as you explore different career options.

Another way to find a good career is to utilize career counseling services or career coaches. Career counselors are trained professionals who can help you explore your options, identify your strengths and interests, and develop a career plan. They can also provide valuable guidance and support as you navigate the job search process, including helping with your resumé and giving you job interview tips and tricks. Career counseling services may be offered by your school or university, community organizations, or private career counseling firms. Career coaches are individuals who listen well, help with assessments, and bridge the gap for you in helping you find the most productive career choice for whatever stage you might be in right now.

Finally, it is important to do your own research and gain real-world experience to find a promising career for yourself. This can include talking to people in the field, researching job requirements and roles, and gaining relevant experience through internships, volunteer work, or other opportunities. Understanding the day-to-day reality of a job can give you a better sense of whether it's a good fit for you and can help you make a more informed decision.

The Most Successful Business Type Might Not Be the Most Glamorous

When choosing your career path, it is important to consider the overall benefit vs. the cost. Is your salary worth the hours? If you are starting and running your own business, will the revenue cover your office rent (if you need a physical place to run that business) and all other expenses, including paying employees, insurance, and additional overhead costs? When deciding on a career, talk to the experts, do the math, and run the figures. Seek to know everything about everything in your career path.

My business success began by selling insurance, which was never very glamorous, especially in the beginning when I had to work evenings and weekends to be available to talk to hard-working men and women. I was always glad to be able to offer them security and comfort in case anything unfortunate happened, but being an insurance salesman was not like being an actor or doctor—there was nothing prestigious about it.

But it paid the bills. It allowed me to grow into a business owner. It eventually allowed me to invest in commercial real estate and hop off the treadmill of working hourly for a paycheck. It was, at the time, a very practical job that fed my family, and I am very grateful that Darryl Nelson gave me the opportunity (see chapter 3 from my first book, *The Right Kind of Rich*).

Choosing to Start a Business

Owning and running your own business can give you the freedom to grow in ways that aren't available to you as an employee. Learning more about your market and understanding ways you can pivot and grow when new opportunities arise can lead to explosive growth.

When you seek to become an expert in the field you choose, you will be better able to understand the business potential and ways you can enhance your revenue streams. If you are reaching just one type of customer with one kind of product, you could become an expert with a second product type and reach a different kind of customer, doubling your customer base. Most good businesses will have ways to increase their revenue streams. My advice is to stay away from the ones that don't.

Also, consider the initial investment and the speed at which you can be profitable. Are you buying into a franchise? How many years will it take to make a profit? Are you thinking about opening a brick-and-mortar store? How long will it take to build a customer base and pay back your start-up investment while paying rent, buying stock, and paying employees? Are you planning on becoming a heavy equipment operator? How many jobs will it take to pay off the backhoe? Be realistic and go into your career choice with your eyes wide open. Hope and positivity are great attributes but not the best strategies. Run the numbers, talk with professionals, and set appropriate goals that you need to reach monthly, quarterly, and annually.

It is not possible to predict every problem that will arise but talking to other people with experience can help give you a clear idea of what could happen, both good and bad. Don't be a doom-and-gloom pessimist, but don't be an optimist with your head in the clouds. Keep your feet on the ground, your head always thinking and planning, and your eyes wide open.

Final Thoughts

According to recent statistics, the success rate of start-up businesses varies depending on the industry and the stage of the business. For example, a study by the Small Business Administration (SBA) found that about 20 percent of new businesses fail within the first year, and about 50 percent fail within the first five years. However, these statistics vary depending on the industry, with some having much higher failure rates than others.

One of the main reasons for start-up failure is the lack of market demand for the product or service. A study by CB Insights found that 42 percent of start-up failures were due to a lack of market need for the product or service. This can happen when entrepreneurs fail to conduct proper market research before starting their businesses. Other reasons for failure include running out of cash (see chapter 5), poor management, and an inability to scale the business.

Despite these challenges, it's worth noting that start-up businesses can also be very successful. A study by the Ewing Marion Kauffman Foundation found that new businesses are responsible for nearly all net new job creation and almost 20 percent of gross job creation.

It's important to remember that starting a business is a high-risk venture and failure rates are relatively high, but with the right business mindset, you can mitigate the risks and pick and start a strong business with good potential. This includes going into a career with the knowledge of what it will cost for training and business investment.

Keep in mind that it may be worth starting off as an employee in the field you've chosen. If you have a long-term mindset, you can spend a couple of years learning the ins-and-outs and the what-to-dos and what-not-to-dos, gaining the knowledge and experience you will need when you step out on your own.

Questions to Ask Yourself:

1. Can this business scale (grow)?

2. Can this be a lifetime business?

3. What technology is being developed in this field?

4. What does the economy look like?

5. What are my strengths and weaknesses?

6. Do I need training or additional skills to do this job?

2

THERE WILL ALWAYS BE SOMETHING TO LEARN

Lifelong learning is an essential part of being successful in life. When you stop learning or think that you know enough, you stop growing as a person and stop your business from growing. There is a reason so many professional service jobs require a certain number of hours for professional development. Everyone needs to keep learning and growing. If you don't keep moving forward and gaining more skills or knowledge, you will eventually become stagnant.

I love knowing everything I can about my business and keeping that knowledge up as my industry changes. I love talking to people who know more than me, asking them questions, and getting their advice. I love geeking out about my industry with others and sharing my knowledge with them.

Sharing with others and constantly learning creates excitement and a desire to know more.

Most people think that my business, self-storage facility ownership, is not a glamorous business. And while it may encourage some people to nod off while listening to the fascinating details of monthly rents, unit sizes and popularity, contract lengths, and electric gate models, I love it. I get excited to share with newcomers to the industry and other business owners about the market, what I look for in a facility I want to acquire, and how I can increase the value as soon as possible. I get enthusiastic about improving my facilities, meeting the local storage needs of an area, offering investment opportunities to others, and educating fellow storage people.

Being willing to learn and grow should not be limited to business owners or entrepreneurs. Everyone—children, teenagers, young adults, McDonald's employees, CEOs, and even retirees—benefits when they look for opportunities to grow personally, professionally, and relationally. If you can adopt an attitude of learning, you will be able to grow and stay on the forefront of your industry.

As an employee, having an attitude of learning at work can help you to improve your skills, be more productive, and increase your chances of moving up the ladder. By continuously learning new skills and gaining knowledge, you become a more valuable employee and can take on more responsibilities. Learning new skills can also help you be more adaptable and resilient in the face of change. As technology and business practices continue to evolve, leaders and team members need to be able to adapt to new ways of working. By developing an attitude of learning, you will be better equipped to navigate unexpected challenges and take advantage of new opportunities.

A consistent attitude of learning can also help to improve communication and teamwork among team members. By learning new skills, each of us can gain a better understanding of the work of our colleagues, which can lead to improved collaboration and cooperation. Learning and skill development allows you to be more confident and will lead to greater opportunities in your career.

Being willing to keep learning as a leader can also help to create a culture of innovation within your organization. Employees who see their superiors learning and growing are encouraged to educate themselves and are more likely to generate new ideas and find creative solutions to problems. Organizations that foster a learning culture are also more likely to attract and retain top talent. Employees are more likely to be engaged and motivated when they are given opportunities to learn and grow.

Learning doesn't usually come from one source. It comes from people, experiences, successes and failures, classes, conferences, reading magazines and emails, books, YouTube, workshops, and Masterminds. We live in an amazing information age where what we need to know can be found, usually for free.

Having a learning mindset can change even a conversation into a learning experience. It can take a business failure and turn it into a know-what-not-to-do-next-time lesson. It can even take a five-year career pivot and turn it into knowledge gained for the next level in your new career.

You Can Get the Equivalent of a College Education Working for a Company

Sitting behind my desk piled high with files, a Diet Pepsi can, my computer, and picture frames filled with my wife and kids grinning at the camera, I hung up the phone in quiet shock. Wow. All of these years, pouring my heart and soul into my job at Blue Shield of Idaho, and they passed me up for the Vice President of Sales position—the one that had been promised to me.

I had worked at Blue Shield of Idaho for four years, and during that time, I had turned their sales and marketing department into a highly profitable and successful division. I had stayed on, earning less than I was worth, working hard, and traveling around the state away from my family for this opportunity that I would now not get.

As I sat there, I decided that I was done. Blue Shield was a dead-end for me. Working for another company with ladder-climbing potential or even going back to work for myself was important, and I knew that my wife, Carla, would love to move closer to her family.

I immediately packed up my briefcase. It was 5 o'clock, and though I usually stayed later, I was ready to go home, talk to Carla, and think about our future together.

It took a while—at least a year—to appreciate what I learned at that company. Being part of such a huge insurance company gave me a lot of real-world education. I now consider and tell others that those four years were my college education. And it was an education without superfluous classes or knowledge. Everything I learned was directly related to my career, either about insurance, working with customers, or good and bad business practices.

I can now confidently tell you that I wouldn't trade those years of learning for anything. The experience I gained allowed me to grow my own business beyond what I thought possible.

Lifelong Learners Find Unique Ways to Be Constantly Learning

When I started looking at investment opportunities, I read everything I could get my hands on. I narrowed my interest down to real estate and, like most people, started looking into rental houses, multi-family units, and commercial properties. But as I kept digging, something about self-storage facilities appealed to me.

Culturally, Americans like stuff. I knew that. And stuff needs to be stored somewhere. But the more I read about self-storage, the more I realized that having storage space wasn't just for people with stuff. It was for expanding businesses that needed more room. It was for families that were transitioning. It was for commercial operations that wanted a smaller brick-and-mortar footprint.

In my research, I also learned that there was an optimal urban demographic that would ensure the success of self-storage facilities. The more I learned, the more I knew that self-storage was the right investment for me.

Before buying my first facility, I subscribed to self-storage magazines, met with owners, and attended conferences. I did everything I could to learn and know as much as possible. And only then did I start looking for a property to buy.

I started with one facility that we would now consider relatively small. After that, it was one more at a time until I had four. With four self-storage facilities in three different states, I could learn what worked and what didn't. I went from self-educating to learning from experience. I didn't stop attending conferences or reading magazines, but I also had experiential learning.

Experiential learning can be challenging, and you have to have the right mindset. So many people get discouraged when something goes wrong. But if you realize that we are all on a learning journey, the only wrong thing you can do is not learn from your mistakes.

Pick yourself up and dust yourself off after a failure.

Tell yourself, "Well, now I know what *not* to do." And don't do it again. That's the key. Learn what not to do and don't do it.

Now, don't get me wrong. Those four facilities did not fail, in fact, they did quite well. I had plenty of it-worked-so-I-am-going-to-keep-doing-it lessons. Learning goes both ways, from success and failure.

Training is another way you can learn. When I started my self-storage business, no one offered training in acquiring facilities. Self-storage was still considered an alternative real estate class, and there was only limited interest in it. It is not like that now. Now you can go to seminars, Masterminds, and training courses—all types of intentional and intensive learning experiences.

And so many of them will set you on the right path to being a successful self-storage owner.

Most careers have training programs. Those courses can help you learn the nitty-gritty of becoming a successful entrepreneur, business owner, or employee.

A learning mindset means understanding that there is always something more to learn. Be willing to keep researching. Free online courses, podcasts, webinars, and how-tos on social media are good ways to keep learning. You can also talk to experts and invest your time and money in more training. I will never know everything about insurance or self-storage, mainly because the economy, culture, and technology are constantly changing.

Mentors and Peers With Experience Can Expand Your Skills

My bosses and mentors along the way were also part of my career success. They poured their wisdom and experience into me. I knew there was always something I could learn from them, so I came to them with questions about business, life, people, and anything else I thought they might know.

Remember that mentors can be found in more than just bosses or business owners. Mentors can be coworkers with experience, parents who have been there and done that, consultants who you pay, or even people on YouTube and podcasts who create videos that teach and share wisdom. If you are always looking for ways to learn and grow, long-term and short-term mentors can be found anywhere.

Mentors can also play a more significant role in your life and career than you may anticipate. Mentors can become investors or business partners. They may become close friends or confidants. They may even start as bosses, teaching you what to do, and over the years, become friends. Dick Wuthrich began that way for me. He was my boss and taught me everything I knew about customers, business, and shoes as a teenager. But over the years, he has become a lifelong friend.

I want to end with a caution. Not everything that mentors say will be good advice. You are still required to evaluate their advice and wisdom, keep the good, and ignore the bad. They are human and therefore able to make mistakes. Consider all the advice you are given as your responsibility. In the end, you are responsible for every decision you make.

Nontraditional Ways to Expand Your Knowledge

Education and learning don't have to be traditional. When I decided to get into the self-storage industry as a sideline to my insurance business in the early 2000s, I attended the two major National Storage Conventions every year. While there, I would go to every workshop that I could. At that point, I was a veteran business guy but knew nothing about the asset class and business of self-storage. I not only left with excellent information but I was pumped and excited to learn the business and jump in with buying a facility or two. I found out going to the top organizations in this field was one of the best ways to learn about the business.

Most industries have their own national conventions. They have speakers and workshops where they offer excellent insights that you don't want to miss. They also usually provide a time when you can ask questions and speak to experts in the field.

Another way to learn and grow in your field or industry is with podcasts. In any industry, you can listen to 50-plus podcasts from experts talking about everything from best practices to mistakes to avoid to the best ways to reach customers.

There are many ways to start or keep learning about your desired or actual business. Masterminds, networking, magazines, books, conventions, and podcasts are some of the options. The most important thing is to make sure you keep your eyes open for opportunities to learn and grow. Expanding your knowledge helps you minimize or avoid mistakes that can be financially devastating or set you back years.

Final Thoughts

I read this crazy article recently about how travel and living in a new place affects your brain. It increases your problem-solving ability, makes you more creative, and even raises your intelligence. Most importantly, new experiences in new places increase self-confidence. I truly believe this. And it's not just traveling that is good for you; it's trying anything different. Every time you try something new, you create new neurological pathways that increase your brain function. You are forced to look at the new situation or problem and analyze it, figuring out how to handle or solve it. You build confidence in your ability to manage many different situations.

How does that help me find a career or know more about my field, you ask? In lots of ways. The best businesspeople are problem-solvers. They think outside the box. They step into situations with the ability to see what's happening and figure out a way to solve it. They understand that people are different and have different worldviews. They trust themselves to be able to help a situation or business problem.

I saw this in myself and my family. My first traveling experience was on my mission to a mostly Spanish-speaking part of Texas. Because I was young, I didn't know what I could or couldn't accomplish. So I dove headfirst into every situation and loved it. I found out that I could learn a second language in six months, meet and get to know new people almost every day, teach and play with kids of all ages, take care of myself, get along with my missionary companions who came and went every few months, and reach and exceed goals set before me. That time had such a huge impact on me that when Carla and I had kids, we desired for them to grow up experiencing and understanding other cultures too.

I believe that travel and new experiences not only make you a better person but really do increase your capacity for learning and problem-solving.

Questions to Ask Yourself:

1. Who can teach me about life and business skills?

2. Who are the mentors/peers in my life/career who I can learn the most from?

3. What conventions can I attend to learn more about my field of business?

4. What podcasts/magazines can I follow to help me be a lifelong learner?

5. How can I get the skills I need to create profitable momentum?

6. What is my plan to continue to learn business skills?

3

WORK HARD WHILE CREATING FUN ALONG THE WAY

Burnout in work and life is a real thing. And avoiding burnout is more complicated than just following a few simple steps. Burnout comes from being focused on the wrong thing, not having a good support system, not feeling fulfilled in your career, being unable to move up or grow professionally, struggling with coworkers or other relationships, dealing with personal issues, or a myriad of other reasons.

Being aware of how you are doing and understanding how you can start feeling fulfilled and encouraged in your job and career are the keys to overcoming or avoiding burnout.

Balancing business and life can be a challenge for many people, including me. It's important to find a balance that works for you so that you can be productive in both areas and not feel overwhelmed.

One way to avoid burnout is to build rhythm and routines into your daily life. Decide on work hours that allow you to be productive while still having time for other things. For example, you might set a rule that you won't work after a certain time each day, or that you won't work on weekends.

Another strategy is to start habits that build on each other. Make a list of what's most important to you in both business and life and allocate time and energy accordingly. For example, if family time is a high priority, make sure you have regular quality time with loved ones and take time off when you need it.

I have found that it is important to balance business and life with your time, mental focus, and energy. Use tools like calendars, task lists, and time-tracking apps to help you stay on top of your responsibilities and work. And don't be afraid to delegate. This can free up time for you to focus on the most important things.

Finding joy and fulfillment helps avoid burnout. Making the necessary changes to your career or shifting your priority and focus can increase your enjoyment of work and help you engage for the long haul.

Finally, knowing yourself, understanding your strengths and weaknesses, and becoming aware of what stresses you can help you know where you need to make changes, add downtime, or find someone to help you with a skill set you might not have.

Build in a Rhythm of Work, Family Time, and Vacations

"Carla! Guess what?!? We did it! We qualified for the cruise!" Grabbing her hands, I did an awkward jump-hop-dance around the kitchen. The grin on her face was almost as big as mine, as she tried to keep up with my off-rhythm jig.

Earlier that year, one of the companies that I sold insurance for had sent out a memo listing the rewards that their brokers could qualify for if they reached a certain level of sales.

I had seen the memo and determined that I would get to the top level and receive an all-expense-paid cruise in the Caribbean. I had worked steadily all year, not pushing or selling that particular insurance carrier to people who didn't need it but working to find the right people who would benefit. I was very passionate about meeting their insurance needs.

Just that afternoon, I got word that we had made it. Instead of calling Carla and telling her on the phone, I decided to pick up flowers and surprise her in person.

At that point, we had only been married for a few years and had not taken a real vacation since our honeymoon. I had not grown up taking vacations. The closest thing I had to a vacation was cutting logs with my uncle when I was young. My cousin and I had slept in hammocks in the mountains outside of their camping trailer. After work, we had been able to fish and cook over a campfire. Carla had been a farmer's daughter. Even though her family could have afforded it, they couldn't leave their fields or animals for more than a night or two. We both saw vacationing as a luxury.

That was the main reason we were so excited. The other reason was that I had worked so hard and it was fulfilling to meet my goals and get to relax and enjoy the fruit of my labor.

I ended up earning vacations regularly as I got more and more successful in insurance. In fact, when our youngest was a teenager, I won three trips to Hawaii in one year! Those trips and incentives taught me that playing was an essential part of living a balanced life.

Being reward-motivated can help to keep you going. Rewards are helpful to keep a focus on pushing you to work hard, do your best, and succeed. And rewards don't have to be from external sources like in the insurance business. You can create your own rewards for the goals you set to reach a certain level, sign a certain number of clients, or work hard on your new business for a certain amount of time.

Having things to anticipate keeps you engaged. It doesn't always have to be a vacation. It could be an item, a financial bonus, or even a few days of hiking and exploring with your kids.

Humans are all reward-motivated. We are rewarded for working hard with a paycheck. We are rewarded for our patience toward our families with strong support systems. We are rewarded for exercising and watching what we eat with strong bodies. We are all motivated by rewards in some form.

We also need something to look forward to at different times and seasons of our life. We need to work hard to save money so we can own a house. We need to look forward to dinner and a movie at the end of a long work week. A family vacation next summer can help us buckle down and get the things done that will fund that fun trip without going into debt.

Working with your human nature and refusing to be a superhero who doesn't have needs will keep you balanced so you can continue to work hard and meet your goals.

Build Habits That Build Balance

I was not always good at balancing my work and play time. When I first got into insurance, both for myself and then later for Blue Shield, I worked too much. Carla was always patient with me, but one time she found a good way to remind me of my priorities.

I had started the habit of popping into my office at Blue Shield in Lewiston, Idaho, for a few hours every Saturday morning before Carla and the kids got up. I spent that time prepping for Monday morning when my team would come in. It helped me stay on top of our objectives and gave me some time to work uninterrupted.

That particular Saturday, I had a few fires that I needed to put out on Monday and I lost track of time, planning how I would address my team. I was interrupted by my office phone ringing. Wondering who would be calling my office extension so early in the morning on a Saturday, I was startled to see that it was already almost noon.

With a sinking feeling, I answered the phone. "Hello, this is Ron Osborne."

"Morning, honey." My wife sounded way too patient. "I was just wondering if you need me to put a cot in your office so you can sleep there when you need a rest."

I knew I was in trouble. Chuckling, I told her, "I'll head home right now. See you soon."

I took her gentle hint to heart. I tended to pour my heart and soul into work, spending long hours at the office. But I had a wife and three children at the time, and they needed to see me on the weekends.

Work-life balance is one important way to avoid burnout and what could be stressful chaos in your life.

Another way to keep from getting burned out is to get on a daily and weekly schedule that works for you. I am a morning person so I have found that if I get up early, I am the most focused and productive before most of the world is even awake. This only works because I go to bed fairly early. My family is used to this and it works for us. I also spend Sundays at home with them. That is the day I set aside for my family no matter what is going on in my work life. Having these habits and routines helps me balance my professional career and my home life.

I also have some hobbies that energize me. I love playing golf. I am very thankful that I was in a business where a lot of transactions happened on the golf course. It combined two of my favorite things. But I also love spending time with my family—especially my kids and grandkids—and close friends. My other energizing activity is leading and interacting with young people at my church. Having these four focuses—work, family, church, and golf—has helped me stay balanced and energized.

On the other hand, things that disrupt the balance of your life should be minimized: destructive habits, unnecessary stress, and unhealthy relationships. Creating boundaries for yourself and your family will foster an atmosphere where peace and joy win out over the stress and pressure of the world.

Balance Business and Life

Every so often, you need to ask yourself what is most important to you. Are you in a season where you feel like focusing on work is important? Do you have obligations outside of work that need to be changed? Is it time to hire an assistant so you can be present at home more? Has work or life slowed down enough that you can focus on a vacation? Does something need to change seriously, like your career or business?

Balancing work and life is hard but possible.

You need to be honest with yourself and your family. And they need to be honest with you. If you don't have a family, ask yourself what you need to balance in order to go the long haul. Find a way to live your life in balance.

One of the ways I did this was by taking my family to a cabin or condo in the mountains every opportunity I could, usually for long weekends. We have so many good memories of riding bikes on the trails, roasting marshmallows over an open fire, singing loudly (and off-key) to the radio on the way up and back, sleeping in on quiet snowy mornings, making big breakfasts, and playing games in the evenings around the fireplace. It really helped me balance my work and family life, the kids loved it, and we grew closer as a family.

Finding Joy and Fulfillment in Your Work

Avoiding burnout is not just about balancing work and fun. Another important focus is doing meaningful work. We can't all be healthcare workers, counselors, or teachers, but we all can find meaningful work.

Insurance doesn't seem meaningful to most people. They think about policies, deductibles, and payments. What they may not think about is the peace of mind that insurance brings to people or the help that policyholders receive in difficult situations—insurance is there to help people when negative events occur. I made sure that we, as their insurance brokers, helped our clients when they needed us. It was meaningful work.

Even now, running a successful self-storage business is meaningful, and not because I provide places for people to store their stuff. It is meaningful because I provide financial and career stability to over 80 people, offer investment opportunities to dozens of others, and create an uplifting and encouraging working environment for my employees and business partners. I focus on the people-impact of my work.

For someone else who is less people focused, they might find fulfillment in problem-solving, in creating a new program that fixes an issue, or in being financially secure themselves. Everybody is different and finding meaningful and fulfilling work is important.

The Importance of Being Fulfilled

Finding or doing work that you *love*, or at least *like* most of the time is extremely important. Most people will work for more than 40 years. If you are miserable, dread going to work, are always dealing with problems or hard coworkers, or work day and night with very little to show for it (fulfillment-wise or financially), you probably need to rethink your business or career.

The COVID pandemic brought a lot of change to the world. One of the major things that it ushered in is often called the Great Resignation. In 2021 and 2022, more people quit their jobs and started another than at any other time in American history (since those records started being kept by the U.S. Bureau of Labor Statistics Job Openings and Labor Turnover Survey program). There is a lot of speculation about the reason people are quitting and changing jobs, but one of the major reasons seems to be fulfillment in the workplace.

An article on the World Economic Forum website, written by Stefan Ellerbeck, explains how this trend is continuing and why.

> *The Great Resignation, a term coined in May 2021, describes the record number of people leaving their jobs since the beginning of the pandemic. After an extended period of working from home with no commute, many people have decided their work-life balance has become more important to them.*
>
> *This revolution in the world of work appears to be continuing apace, with one in five workers globally planning to quit in 2022. That's the key finding of consultancy firm PwC's Global Workforce Hopes and Fears Survey of more than 52,000 workers in 44 countries and territories, carried out in March 2022. It says pay is unsurprisingly the main factor in people wanting to change jobs, with 71 percent citing it as a key reason.*
>
> *Yet money isn't enough by itself to retain workers, who were almost as likely to cite intangible factors related to meaning. Job fulfillment and the ability to be one's true self at work were ranked second and third among employees considering a job change.*

That study was conducted in 44 different countries. That means that fulfillment is a universal desire in people of all nationalities, not just an American one.

Increasing Your Self-Awareness

How's it going? We hear that question every day and forget that it's a question. In our culture, it means hi. But take a moment and think about the question. How *are* you doing? Are you feeling fulfilled or frustrated? Are you weary or energized? Are you reactive or calm? How do you handle stress? How do you de-stress? In what ways can you continue to grow? What makes you feel good? What makes you feel *ugh*?

Being self-aware is very important. It is more than just knowing your strengths and weaknesses. It is about evaluating your actions, motivations, and feelings.

Feelings are a thermometer. They tell you how hot or cold you are. They are not the reason for the temperature, and they are not the truth of a situation—they are just a gauge to help you be self-aware.

The more situations I experienced as a business owner, the more perspective I gained.

Especially now, I can get frustrated, angry, or excited about a situation but know that those emotions reflect on me, not necessarily the situation. I found that I needed to look at the situation rationally to understand the pros and cons, the potential returns or problems, and the long-term consequences no matter how excited or anxious I was about it.

We recently had an opportunity to acquire a large number of self-storage facilities in one transaction. We started the due diligence process and I was cautiously excited. They looked good and had a lot of potential to add value almost immediately. They would have also increased our commercial real estate portfolio by a huge amount and taken us one step closer to our goal number of total owned properties.

We continued the process, and I became more and more excited about the possibilities. Thankfully, right before we closed, we found out that what the sellers claimed to pay in property taxes was way off from what the three firms we hired to double-check everything said we would be paying. It was off by millions of dollars. It was a huge red flag and could potentially mean the difference between making a profit or taking a loss. Even though it killed me to do it, we decided to pull out and not purchase this group of properties.

It is important to understand that just because you are excited about something doesn't make it the right thing to do. And the opposite is true too. Being anxious or nervous about something doesn't mean you shouldn't go ahead with it. You need to rely on logic, research, and wisdom.

Final Thoughts

Over my many years in business and working with people, not just customers and clients, but bosses, employees, and partners, I learned that the better you understand yourself, your emotions, and your strengths and weaknesses, the better you can change or adjust your lifestyle to create a long-term, sustainable focus in your business, career, or work life. Knowing what makes you tick or what drains your energy can open opportunities to add or subtract a habit from your life.

Taking time off to relax, have fun, connect with your family, friends, and community, and focus on something besides work will allow you to go the long haul with your career. Making the right career choices, including what companies you choose to work for, is not just about plugging along steadily year after year. It is also about enjoying what you are doing, feeling fulfilled in your work or hobbies, making a difference in others' lives, and having vision for the future.

Questions to Ask Yourself:

1. How do you know what personal systems to be consistent about as a business owner?

2. Why is work/play balance important for business success?

3. How do I create a balanced life if it's never been modeled for me?

4. What do I like to do outside of work?

5. How am I doing right now?

6. What can I change about my life so I can feel more balanced?

4

LIVE DIFFERENTLY AND INVEST THE REST

We live in a day and age where most people are maxed out, financially, emotionally, physically, and relationally. The huge problem is that they don't have anything extra to give when it is required, especially financially.

Recently a survey came out that showed that 65 percent of Americans are living paycheck to paycheck.

If they have an emergency or can't work, they can't pay their bills. They have no savings or investments they can fall back on when they are in desperate times.

I grew up like this and know what it is like. It's why I am motivated to share my stories and let others know there are opportunities all around them that they might not be able to see. Growing up, we lived paycheck to paycheck, especially after my father passed away when I was 10 years old. It was a regular occurrence when I was little that my parents were not able to buy groceries at the end of the month and were holding their breath until they were paid again. And when my dad had his stroke, we were desperate. After he died, my mom struggled to pay our bills and even had to get a personal loan from a family member so we could go to the dentist. Every curveball that life threw at us threatened to make us homeless.

Because of these difficulties, I constantly challenge young people to be different. Do the hard thing and live within your means. Budget your paycheck and make sure you can put some away. Be different from the 65 percent of Americans who live paycheck to paycheck or worse, the 55 percent of Americans who also have credit card debt.

Living within your means is a key aspect of financial stability and security. It means understanding your income and expenses and making sure that you are spending less than you earn. This can be done by creating a budget and tracking your spending, as well as by avoiding unnecessary expenses and looking for ways to cut back on your spending.

One of the most important things you can do to live within your means is to save a portion of your income. By setting aside a certain percentage of your income each month, or by setting a specific savings goal, you'll be better able to handle unexpected expenses and have a cushion for emergencies.

Another key aspect of living on what you make from your job or business is to avoid taking on too much debt. This means being mindful of your credit card and loan balances and working to pay them off as quickly as possible. High levels of debt can make it difficult to save, let alone have enough money to invest, and can also be a source of personal stress.

Once you have established a habit of living within your means, you can start to place the rest of your money in investments that align with your financial goals.

When I started looking into different investment options, real estate—such as rental properties, office buildings, and self-storage facilities—was an excellent way to generate income and grow my wealth over time. However, I knew it was important to understand the costs and responsibilities associated with property ownership and to invest only what I could afford.

Finally, it's important to remember that investing is a long-term strategy and you need to be patient. By living within your means and investing the rest, you can build a solid foundation for your financial future.

Keep an Eye on Your Finances

The first step to achieving financial stability and security is keeping an eye on your monthly finances.

Being aware of what comes in and what goes out (gets spent), allows you to have a clear picture of your financial situation. Knowing your income, expenses, assets, and liabilities gives you a good understanding of your current financial position, and allows you to make decisions about spending, saving, and investing.

Staying in the know about your finances can also help you to identify and address financial problems early on. By keeping track of your spending and regularly reviewing your statements and bills, you can spot discrepancies or fraudulent activity, and act quickly to prevent any financial losses.

Being financially aware helps you to create and stick to a budget. By understanding your expenses, you can create a realistic budget that takes into account your income, expenses, and financial goals. This can help you to prioritize your spending and avoid overspending, save more, and reach your financial goals sooner.

Managing your money can help you to plan for the future. By understanding your current financial situation, you can plan for retirement, college education for your children, or any other long-term goals you may have.

Finally, keeping tabs on your financials can provide peace of mind. Knowing that you are in control of your finances and have a plan in place can reduce stress and anxiety, allowing you to focus on other important aspects of your life.

Think Big Picture From the Beginning

When Carla and I were planning our wedding and our life together, we had many conversations about our finances. I was thankful that Carla grew up financially stable and knew the value of money and hard work. She didn't like to spend money frivolously and valued saving a portion of her paycheck.

We talked about how amazing it would be to live on my paycheck and save hers. Now before you tell me that it was a different time, this was the early 80s when interest rates were 18.6

percent. We did the math and decided that we probably wouldn't ever be able to own a house.

Over the next year or two, we changed our minds and decided that it would be worth buying a house if we could pay off the mortgage as quickly as possible. While Carla had a job, before we had kids, we put her paycheck away to save it for our down payment. When we finally found a cute little house in Burley, Idaho, we were able to buy it and used our savings for the down payment.

By that time, I was making enough money to also put some of my paycheck away for emergencies. Because of our frugalness, we were able to pay down our mortgage and had a small emergency fund.

Our smart financial decisions allowed us to prioritize what we valued most. Carla was able to stay home to be there for the kids while I worked.

People have different priorities: starting their own business, traveling a good portion of the year, retiring early, moving to another country, adopting children, being able to help others financially, or even starting a nonprofit organization. Every one of these priorities takes money. And lack of money or debt can and will hold you back.

Thinking about the big picture can help you achieve your goals.

Keeping the end in mind will help you make sacrifices for the reward of meeting your goal. Living beneath your means is about much more than money. Yes, it includes lowering your budget so you can save money each month. But it also means positioning yourself to be ready to take the next step to meet your goals and fulfill your dream.

One of my goals and values was to be financially stable. I needed and wanted to be able to take care of my own family but also help my mom and siblings. I was able to do this a bit through the years, but I knew that something big needed to happen in order to help our community on a larger scale.

After I had started my business Western Benefits Solution (WBS) in 1997, we had enough savings that I began looking for ways to invest the money. This was possible because we had always lived beneath our means. I eventually found four self-storage facilities in the early 2000s with good growth and profit potential. Once we got these facilities running smoothly, we could pay off the loan with the cash flow they created because I made more than enough at WBS. We never had to live off the income of the self-storage investments.

Those four facilities did so well that when I transitioned away from insurance after selling WBS, I created a company with my oldest son, AJ, and son-in-law, Sam, that bought, transformed, and managed self-storage facilities. Bitterroot Holdings helped me meet and exceed my goals and vision through commercial real estate investing.

Sacrifice for Your Goals

I want to get practical for a minute. Telling people to follow their dreams is too pie-in-the-sky. How do we achieve the goals that help us stick to our values?

Start by identifying your priorities or dreams and why you want to accomplish them. Here are some examples:

- I want to be a stay-at-home mom to be the one to raise my kids.
- I want to have a mobile job so I can live in different countries.
- I want to buy and pay off a house to have financial freedom when I'm older.
- I want to start a nonprofit organization that helps underprivileged youth with school and tutors.
- I want to be able to retire early and enjoy my later years.

Whatever your goal, it is important to be deliberate about taking the next steps. Ask yourself what steps must be taken. List the things that you need to take those next steps, such as a certain amount of passive income, language fluency, training in a specific field, an investment opportunity, a partner with certain skills, and other things that come to mind.

Last of all, start doing what you can. Make small changes. They will add up to significant changes. If you can make big steps, do it. You want to be moving toward your goals consistently, no matter the size of the step. If you can keep your eyes on where you want to end up, you can stay motivated to sacrifice for your long-term goals.

Keep Evaluating Quarter by Quarter and Year by Year

Money goals are not something that you figure out today and forget about tomorrow. Money goals need to be evaluated multiple times a year. If you have a spouse, you need to set money goals together. Only with your eyes open can you see, evaluate, and change your financial trajectory.

It is extremely important to know what money is coming in, where it is going, and how much is left at the end of every month. Keeping a budget is an excellent way to limit unnecessary spending. A budget doesn't have to be painful. It can include sections for entertainment, charitable giving, and even a clothes budget. It is up to you to decide where you want your money to go. Just make sure you do it deliberately. This can help you stay on track to achieve your financial goals and avoid costly mistakes.

One of the most effective ways to evaluate your finances is to do so on a quarterly basis. This allows you to track your progress throughout the year and make any necessary adjustments in a timely manner. For example, if you find that you are spending more than you expected in a particular category, such as dining out or entertainment, you can take steps to reduce that expense in the next quarter.

Evaluating your finances on a yearly basis is also important. This allows you to see the bigger picture and identify long-term trends. For example, if you find that your income has been increasing over the past several years, you may want to consider increasing your savings or investment contributions. On the other hand, if your expenses have been steadily increasing, you may want to take steps to reduce them.

Another essential aspect of evaluating your finances on a yearly basis is to reassess your financial goals. It's important to make sure that your goals are still realistic and aligned with your current financial situation. This can help you stay motivated and focused on achieving your goals.

One thing that people don't consider often is insurance coverage. Reviewing your homeowners, car, medical, and—if needed for your business—your liability coverage yearly can make a huge difference when you actually need them. It's unfortunate, but we live in a time and place where cars hit something they shouldn't, pipes leak, and businesses get sued.

It's important to seek professional advice when evaluating your finances and financial goals. A financial adviser can provide valuable guidance and help you develop a plan to help you get to where you want to be financially. They can also help you identify potential risks and opportunities, which can help you make more informed decisions about your finances.

Generate Income in Unexpected Places

When I first looked into self-storage, it was considered an alternative asset class. The "real" investors wouldn't even consider it. That has all changed. By investing in self-storage facilities, I was doing what some people would consider risky or outside the box. I didn't care. I ran my own numbers and decided that it was worth the try. This risky investment has turned out to be a great win for my family and me.

What out-of-the-box ideas do you have to generate income? How about your spouse? Do they have ideas, assets, or abilities you could use to grow financially? The best entrepreneurs think of different and unconventional ways to move forward toward their goals and dreams.

One way to generate income in unexpected ways is through renting out a spare room on Airbnb or even as a long-term rental. This can be a great way to earn extra money by utilizing space that is not being used in your home. It could also allow you to meet people from all over the world and potentially make new friends.

Another unique way to generate income is through online tutoring or teaching. With the rise of online learning platforms, there are many opportunities to teach a variety of subjects to students of all ages. This can be done on a part-time or full-time basis and can be a great way to earn money while sharing your knowledge and expertise.

Jobs such as driving for Uber or Lyft, delivering food or packages for companies like GrubHub or DoorDash, or even working as a freelancer in a specific field can also generate income. It may be the side hustle that sets you up as you get a business started.

Creating and selling online courses or digital products can be another great way to generate income. This can include ebooks, printables, templates, or even online classes or workshops. Think about skills you have that others need to monetize your expertise and share your knowledge with others.

Selling items on online marketplaces like eBay, Amazon, or Etsy can be another way to bring in monthly income. This can include items that you no longer need or want, or even items that you create yourself.

There are many other ways to bring in some extra income if you get creative and think outside the box. You are only limited by your time and energy.

Final Thoughts

Living paycheck to paycheck can limit your ability to enjoy life. Without the ability to save for vacations, hobbies, or other leisure activities, it can be difficult to relax and enjoy life outside of work. It makes it difficult to achieve financial stability and security and plan for the future.

Don't discount the peace of mind that financial stability brings. When you are always worrying about how to pay the rent, if you'll have enough money at the end of the month for food, or what will happen if you get sick, you miss the ability to enjoy the here and now.

Keep in mind that it's not all about vacations and four-wheelers. It's about having financial security knowing that if something unexpected happens, you and your family will be ok; when your family car breaks down, you can fix or replace it; and you have money to live on when life doesn't go perfectly.

I started working when I was young, not because I had nothing better to do, but because I needed money. And I have worked consistently since then. My financial goals are no longer to help my mom with groceries, afford a milkshake, or buy a pair of cool sneakers. They have grown with me and my business. But they still take sacrifice and discipline. I found out as a kid that not spending my whole paycheck was worth it in the long run. And today, almost 50 years later, the same applies, though my goals are a bit bigger than a pair of new shoes.

Questions to Ask Yourself:

1. What is your big-picture financial goal?

2. What are the smaller steps that can get you there?

3. What needs to happen to make saving a large portion of your earnings possible?

4. In what ways can you invest now?

5. What sacrifices can you make now to improve your future?

6. What other jobs can you do to generate extra income?

5

IT IS VITAL TO UNDERSTAND THE IMPORTANT DETAILS OF BUSINESS

Someone recently asked me how many Limited Liability Companies (LLC) I have started over my career. After a quick mental addition, I guessed the figure to be between 50 and 75. What people don't realize is that each of those LLCs is a business unto itself.

Thankfully, in America, starting a business is not hard.

Many people have turned a side job into a career. Starting a mowing business on the weekends and after school can turn into a full-time, year-round lawn, garden, tree-trimming, and snow-removal business. For me, it started with a suit, tie, briefcase, a comfortable pair of shoes, and a plan to walk door to door, talking to people about insurance. I went from a one-man operation to eventually selling my insurance business for well over six figures and diving headfirst into commercial real estate.

My story and history is not an anomaly. I am the typical story of starting small, doing things right or learning when I did them wrong, being smart about business decisions, and working hard. Along the way, I had some luck. But I believe it is more about starting in the right business in the right way.

During the early and middle part of my career, listening to and taking business advice was my priority. I didn't have business-savvy parents growing up, but I did find businesspeople with expertise and experience that I could listen to and go to for advice, even as a teenager. And I made sure to take advantage of those opportunities. I encourage individuals at every level to ask, listen and implement. The advice from mentors wasn't just about customer relations or creating rapport with clients. It was also about the super practical aspects of starting and running a business, picking a business name, starting an LLC, the importance of cash flow, finding professional help, putting together a business plan, and understanding marketing, among many others.

I am thankful to be able to offer business advice today from my five decades of work experience, my two different career tracks, and the try-and-learn situations that I have walked through personally.

Types of Businesses

There are many different types of businesses that you can start. Each has different rules and tax implications. It is important to understand the different types of business structures and how they are filed with the government. The following are some common types of business structures.

- **Sole proprietorship:** A business owned and run by a single individual who is personally liable for all debts and obligations. These businesses are easy to set up and typically do not require any formal paperwork to be filed with the government.
- **Partnership:** A business owned by two or more individuals who share profits and liabilities. Partnerships can be general partnerships or limited partnerships and typically require filing a partnership agreement with the state.
- **LLC:** A business structure that combines a corporation's personal liability protection with a partnership's tax benefits. It is basically a company that takes the liability away from the owner in case it is sued. LLCs are simple to form by filing articles of organization with the state.
- **Corporation:** A separate legal entity owned by shareholders, who elect a board of directors to manage the business. Corporations can be either for-profit or nonprofit and typically require filing articles of incorporation with the state.
- **S-Corp**: A corporation that chooses to be taxed under Subchapter S of the Internal Revenue Code. This allows the business income to be passed through to the shareholders rather than taxed at the corporate level.

Even if you are barely starting out in business, creating an LLC (limited liability company) is the way to go. It's something the U.S. government set up decades ago to protect individuals in relation to their business interests and give them some tax advantages too. Forming an LLC is not a difficult process, so you can start there and build momentum.

The Whys and Benefits of an LLC

Forming an LLC is a great way to protect your personal assets while still enjoying the benefits of running your own business. There are a few key benefits of an LLC.

1. Personal liability protection: One of the biggest benefits of an LLC is that it limits your personal liability for the debts and obligations of the business. This means that if your LLC gets sued, your personal assets (like your house or car) will generally be safe from creditors.
2. Tax flexibility: LLCs have the option to be taxed as a sole proprietorship, partnership, or corporation. This means you can choose the tax structure that makes the most sense for your business.
3. Easy to set up: Compared to other business structures like corporations, LLCs are relatively easy to set up. All you need to do is file articles of organization with your state government and pay a small fee.
4. Simple to manage: LLCs have fewer formalities than corporations, this makes them easy to manage and can be run with less paperwork.
5. Attractive to investors: LLCs are a beneficial option for investors, as it provides them with the protection of limited liability while still allowing them to participate in the management of the company.

Overall, forming an LLC can be a great way to start your own business while keeping your personal assets safe. It's a good idea to consult with a legal professional to make sure that an LLC is the best structure for your specific business.

An LLC, or limited liability company, is a popular choice for small businesses and start-ups because it is relatively easy to set up and maintain, and it provides a high level of flexibility in terms of management and operations.

Forming an LLC is fairly simple. It should take only the following three steps:

Step One: Go to the current website of the secretary of state for the state you wish to start the business in (normally, it is the same one you live in). Even if it's an e-commerce business, it may be easiest to form a business in your home state.

If filing in your state is expensive or too complicated, you may file in a state like Wyoming, Delaware, or Nevada, which allow any business to file in their state.

Step Two: Determine a name for your LLC that won't conflict with other business names.

A business of any size can be an LLC and it is a popular business legal structure especially for small companies and start-ups. Similar to getting the right domain name, you should put a little thought into the name of your LLC (although the name of your LLC and your business name can differ).

The main thing you should know is that an LLC helps shield a business owner's assets from business debts if a business should face a lawsuit.

Step Three: Register your LLC with the secretary of state where the business will be run or where your registered agent company will receive mail for your LLC. You will need to pay a relatively small fee. In the state of Idaho, it's $100 to start an LLC and in most states it's in that price range. Once registration is complete, your paperwork will typically be emailed to you and will also be available through your state's business portal. It can usually be mailed to your register's agent's address for an additional fee.

A registered agent company, a law firm, or other services can do these three steps for you, however they typically charge $400 to $1,000, including the state's fee for LLC registration.

Understanding Cash Flow

Cash flow is the movement of money in and out of a business and is one of the most important aspects of financial management. It refers to the amount of money that is coming into a business from sales and other sources, and the amount of money that is going out of the business to pay expenses.

There are several reasons why positive cash flow is important in a business.

First of all, it helps the business meet its financial obligations: A business needs to have enough cash on hand to pay its bills and expenses as they come due. If the business does not have sufficient cash flow, it may struggle to pay its bills and may even default on its loans, with serious consequences.

Second, insufficient cash flow affects the business's ability to grow. A business that has a positive cash flow has the resources to invest in growth opportunities, such as hiring new employees, purchasing new equipment, or expanding into new markets. On the other hand, a business with negative cash flow will struggle to take advantage of these opportunities and may even have to cut back on its operations.

Next, it can impact the business's creditworthiness. A business's cash flow is one of the factors that lenders and investors consider when evaluating the business's creditworthiness. A business with strong cash flow is more likely to be approved for loans and other forms of financing.

Finally, a stunted cash flow can affect the business's ability to weather economic downturns: A business with a strong cash flow has the financial resources to ride out tough times and continue operating until conditions improve.

There are several ways a business can manage its cash flow to ensure that it remains healthy. These include:

Monitoring expenses: A business should regularly review its expenses to identify areas where it can cut costs and reduce the amount of money going out of the business.

Improving collections: A business can improve its cash flow by ensuring that it is collecting payments from customers in a timely manner. This can be done by setting clear payment terms, following up on overdue payments, and offering incentives for timely payment.

Increasing sales: Increasing sales by finding new customers, upselling to existing customers, or launching new products or services is another way to improve cash flow.

Seeking additional financing: If a business is struggling with cash flow, it may be able to improve its situation by seeking additional financing. This can include loans, lines of credit, or investments from outside sources, though without an increase in cash from customers, borrowing money should be done with careful consideration.

As you can see, cash flow is an important aspect of financial management for businesses of all sizes. It plays a crucial role in a business's ability to meet its financial obligations, grow, and remain financially healthy. By closely monitoring and managing your cash flow, you can ensure you have the financial resources you need to be successful day-to-day, month over month.

Getting Professional Help With the Practical Aspects of Your LLC and Cash Flow

Developing a strong foundation of business skills can help you make informed decisions and manage your business more effectively. This can ultimately lead to better financial performance and help you minimize stress. Building relationships with good certified public accountants (CPAs) and other professionals can also be beneficial, as they can provide valuable guidance and support as you grow your business. It's imperative that the professionals you choose are a good fit for the stage your business is at and are willing to grow with you.

A CPA can help you with financial planning and tax strategy, which can save you time and reduce your stress. When interviewing a CPA for tax planning or advice, if they are not able to provide clarity and answers to your questions, keep looking for other CPAs that are well informed. Not all CPAs have expertise in the areas of tax strategy for your particular business.

Other professionals such as lawyers or business consultants can provide advice and support on a range of issues related to running a business. By building a network of trusted advisers, you can have a go-to resource for help and support as you navigate the challenges of growing your business. Take your time in choosing the team members you want to bring around you and work with them to pay what you can afford now and increase the budget as you are more profitable year after year.

Finding good professional help will protect your business in the long term. And there are other important business strategies to keep in mind that will create a good foundation from the inside as you develop your business and its goals.

Business Plan

A well-written business plan is essential for any business. It doesn't have to be complicated but should outline your business idea, financial projections, and strategies for growth and success. As you get into the business, it should be updated regularly.

The first step in creating a business plan is to define your business idea and goals clearly. This includes identifying the problem you're solving, your unique selling point, and what success looks like for your business. Having a clear understanding of these elements will guide the rest of the planning process.

The next crucial part of creating a business plan is understanding the market and industry where your business will operate. Research your target customers, competitors, and potential demand for your product or service. This information will be essential for creating realistic financial projections and identifying opportunities for growth.

Another key component of any business plan is the financials section. Though this can seem complicated, it doesn't have to be. However, it should include creating realistic financial projections. These projections should be based on your research of the market and industry and take into account your business goals.

Your business plan should also include a description of your marketing and sales strategy. I will talk more about this in the next section.

Finally, a business plan should not only describe your business idea and goals but also include an action plan for achieving them. This includes identifying specific milestones and a timeline for achieving them, as well as outlining the resources (financial, human, and technological) that will be needed to execute the plan. This will help you stay on track and make adjustments as needed.

Marketing and Sales Strategy

Developing a solid marketing and sales strategy is critical to the success of your business. This includes identifying your target audience, developing a brand, and finding ways to reach and engage potential customers.

One of the most important steps in developing a marketing and sales strategy is identifying your target audience. This includes understanding their demographics, interests, and pain points. Once you know who your target audience is, you can tailor your marketing and sales efforts to reach and engage them effectively.

Next, developing a strong brand that resonates with your target audience is critical to the success of your marketing and sales efforts. Your brand is the perception that people have of your company. This includes creating a logo, tagline, and overall visual aesthetic that reflects your company's values and mission.

Another essential tool for reaching and engaging customers is digital marketing. This includes tactics such as search engine optimization, social media marketing, email marketing, and content marketing. By effectively utilizing digital marketing, you can reach a large audience and effectively track the success of your marketing efforts.

Finally, measuring and analyzing the success of your marketing and sales efforts is vital to understand what's working and what's not. Use tools such as Google Analytics and social media analytics to track the performance of your campaigns and make data-driven decisions to improve your strategy.

The Importance of Insurance

One of the necessary steps that people seem to forget or put off when they first start a business is getting the right kind of insurance. Unfortunately, if you wait to think about getting insurance until something happens, it's too late.

Directors and officers liability insurance, property insurance, and general liability insurance are the three most important insurances to get. They each cover different things and depending on your business type, you may need one, two, or all three.

Directors and officers liability insurance (D&O) is a special kind of insurance that helps protect the directors and officers, as well as the company itself. This protection is helpful when they're facing legal claims or financial losses because of decisions they've made while running the company.

People can file claims against company leaders for different reasons. If they think there's been some kind of mismanagement, dishonesty, or just bad decision-making, shareholders, employees, customers, and even regulators might file a lawsuit.

D&O insurance covers the cost of defending against these claims, and it can even help pay for settlements or judgments if the company leaders are found to be at fault. However, it doesn't cover everything—if someone's caught doing something illegal on purpose, D&O insurance won't help.

Property insurance for businesses is a type of insurance policy designed to protect a company's physical assets, such as buildings, equipment, furniture, inventory, and other physical property, from various risks and potential financial losses. These risks can include events like fires, theft, vandalism, and natural disasters like storms, floods, or earthquakes.

Property insurance usually covers the actual structure of the business premises, including any owned or leased buildings, and can also include structures like fences, outdoor signs, or landscaping. The coverage helps repair or replace the building if it is damaged or destroyed by a covered event.

It also covers the items inside the building, such as office equipment, machinery, furniture, inventory, and supplies. In case these items are damaged, destroyed, or stolen due to a covered event, the policy helps cover the cost of repairing or replacing them.

When selecting property insurance for a business, it's important to consider factors like the location, nature of the business, the value of the property, and the potential risks involved. It's also essential to review the policy's coverage limits, exclusions, and deductibles to ensure the policy provides adequate protection for the business's specific needs.

General liability insurance covers a variety of things: someone slipping in the gravel walkway to your building and hurting themselves, a gate closing on a car and denting the roof, a leaky pipe in a house where you just installed a dishwasher, your lawnmower sucking up a stone and throwing it into the window of the neighbor's home while you are mowing, or any other simple thing someone could sue you for.

General liability insurance has saved my business in the past and even recently. We had a delinquent renter in one of our self-storage units. We went through the whole legal process to get them either out or caught up on payments. When the process was done and they had not removed their property, we auctioned it off.

Two months later, they reached out with a lawyer and demanded their property which they claimed was worth a sizable amount of money. We referred it to our liability insurance carrier and besides providing them with the eviction paperwork, were able to walk away and leave the headache and problem to the insurance company. It was one of many times when I was deeply thankful for liability insurance.

There are several more types of insurance that are important for businesses to consider, as they can help protect against various risks and potential financial losses. Here's a rundown of some other key insurance types that businesses should think about.

Professional liability insurance (errors and omissions): This insurance is designed for businesses that provide professional services or advice. It covers claims of negligence, errors, or omissions in the services provided, which can lead to financial losses for clients.

Workers' compensation insurance: This insurance is required by law in most states and provides medical, rehabilitation, and wage replacement benefits to employees who are injured or become ill as a result of their job.

Commercial auto insurance: If a business owns or operates vehicles for work purposes, commercial auto insurance is essential. It covers liability and physical damage for vehicles used in the course of business operations.

Business interruption insurance: This type of insurance helps cover lost income and additional expenses when a business is unable to operate due to a covered event, like a natural disaster or major equipment breakdown.

Cyber liability insurance: With the increasing reliance on technology, cyber insurance has become more important. This coverage helps businesses deal with the financial consequences of data breaches, hacking, and other cyber threats.

Employment practices liability insurance (EPLI): This coverage protects businesses against claims related to employment practices like discrimination, harassment, wrongful termination, and other employee-related issues.

Product liability insurance: For businesses that manufacture or sell products, this insurance covers claims related to product defects or malfunctions that cause injury or property damage.

Every business is unique, so it's essential to evaluate the specific risks and needs of the company to determine the most suitable types and levels of insurance coverage. Consulting with an experienced insurance agent or broker can be helpful in making these decisions.

Final Thoughts

Even though many businesses start small, it is extremely important to give them the right foundation. Protecting yourself with LLCs, understanding cash flow, taking the steps to find professional tax or accounting services, creating a business plan, researching the best way to market, and getting the right kind of insurance all create a firm foundation for any type of business.

And if you feel inadequate to do any of these things, there is an amazing free resource that can help you learn and gain the skills needed: YouTube. YouTube has every tutorial imaginable from filing an LLC with your state to learning how to input an expense in QuickBooks and everything in between. You name it and you can learn it.

Try it now. Open your browser and type in: *YouTube creating a business plan for a drive-through coffee shop* or whatever business you are interested in starting. You will be able to look through tutorial after tutorial showing ideas and strategies for starting and running any type of business you want.

Remember to do your research, don't believe everything everyone says, and understand the cost. Once you have pinned down your idea, start with a solid business foundation.

Questions to Ask Yourself:

1. What will the formation of an LLC do for my business?

2. How will learning foundational business skills and developing relationships with a good CPA and other professionals escalate my business and minimize my stress?

3. Why is understanding cash flow an essential business skill?

4. How can a business plan help me plan my business growth?

5. What are the best ways to market my business?

6. What kind of insurance do I need for my particular business?

6

MAKE OTHERS FEEL IMPORTANT IN EVERY INTERACTION

As I put back the eighth pair of rejected shoes in their vacant place on the wooden shelf in the back of the store, I sighed in frustration. Mrs. Lewis was always a picky customer. She hardly ever found something she liked, yet she kept coming back.

I knew that one of the problems was that she was in denial about her shoe size. I didn't understand why women were embarrassed about having size 9 or 10 feet. I knew that most women wanted small feet, but I didn't understand why for the life of me. But then again, most women puzzled me, including my sister. I rolled my eyes just thinking about her taste in boyfriends as I forced my mind back to finding a solution for Mrs. Lewis.

Thinking about all the shoes she had chosen and discarded, I found a theme. She liked a pointed toe and low heel. She also liked dark-colored shoes, but I remembered that she kept glancing at a pair of bright sunflower yellow sandals, though she hadn't dared to try them on.

I quickly considered and then rejected our most popular shoes. The Charley pumps? Too high. The Monna T-back flats? Probably not. And then I thought about the gray Thomas Jans with the open-back T-strap. They might work! The toes were pointed, the heels low, and most importantly, their sizes ran big. She could probably fit the size 8.

I grabbed the shoe box and then found another pair in brown. Hesitating over a third pair, I decided to push my luck and grabbed a pair in red suede as well. I quickly returned to Mrs. Lewis with a grin on my face. "Mrs. Lewis, I think I have exactly what you are looking for."

When I returned to the store 45 minutes later, after carrying Mrs. Lewis's purchase to her car—two pairs of shoes for herself and a pair for her daughter—I looked at the grinning Mr. Wuthrich. "Wow, nice job, Ronnie. You just got us a customer for life."

Learning how to talk to customers and meet their needs by finding shoes they didn't know they needed was excellent training for me as a teenager. I used those skills later to understand my clients' needs and help them find the right insurance.

Some people may wonder what shoes have in common with selling insurance. I would answer: people. Those years I worked at Hudson Shoe Store began my learning about life, culture, people, and business.

The shoe store job also taught me consistency, hard work, being teachable, handling difficult clients, self-motivation, and personal finance. Those things helped make me who I was as I started my career and who I am today.

Customers were my bread and butter for almost 40 years. My business was based on customer service, first as a shoe salesman and later as an insurance salesman. A lot of things have changed over those four decades, but people are still people.

Most businesses are customer based, and it is vital to understand how to reach and keep those customers. People want to be heard, have their needs met, and be appreciated. It is that simple.

Build Relationships and Friendships That Last

If you are in or own a service-based business, clients are the company's lifeblood. Relationships are the key to business. Meeting, getting to know, and connecting with your clients will ensure they stay.

Connecting with clients is not about faking it.

People are too smart for that. It reminds me of the restaurant host who is required to ask how your day is going while leading you to your seat. First, they are facing the wrong way, so you have difficulty hearing them. Second, how realistic is it to try and connect in the less than a minute while your whole party is walking through the loud restaurant?

On the other hand, the server has a perfect opportunity to connect. And good servers do. They find out a bit about you and you about them. They make you feel appreciated and welcome. They anticipate your needs and help with any problems that may arise. And in turn, you want to leave them a good tip and sit in their section the next time.

Connecting and building relationships were my favorite things about insurance. I genuinely enjoy getting to know new people. I would find something to connect with them about, hear their needs, and learn how to prioritize the right insurance solution.

Due to my line of work, I could take potential clients to lunch or dinner, play golf with them, or offer them box seats to football games. Each of these things would connect us and continue to build our relationships. It's an authentic way to do it and causes customers to see you as a business solution, professional resource, and friend.

Asking Questions and Listening are Essential Skills to Experience Business Growth and Life Satisfaction

There are many aspects to building relationships with your customers. Two of the most underrated communication skills are asking questions and genuinely listening. These things go hand in hand when creating connections and building relationships, not just with your customers but with everybody.

The Power of Questions

Questions reach people on two levels. They show others that you are genuinely interested in them, their lives, and their interests, and they also allow you to explore areas where you can help them and meet their needs.

Using questions goes way beyond just getting to know people. It can spur learning and the exchange of ideas, it can lead to innovation and performance improvement, and if done correctly, it can build rapport and trust within relationships. It can also uncover pitfalls and potential problems in a business.

For some people, asking questions comes easily. Their natural curiosity, emotional intelligence, and ability to read people help them form the perfect line of questions that provide the right information needed. However, a good majority of people don't know the right questions to ask, ask enough questions, or pose those questions in the right way. This can lead to insufficient knowledge and therefore imperfect solutions.

The good news is that everyone can practice and improve their question-asking skills. And the more you do it, the better you get.

Dale Carnegie told people in his classic business book *How to Win Friends and Influence People*, "Ask questions the other person will enjoy answering." Asking invasive or difficult questions can uncover revealing answers, but it will not encourage continued relationships. Asking people about what they love, are excited about, or even their latest challenge that they want to talk about encourages relationship building.

There are many reasons why people don't ask questions. It could be because they are self-focused and waiting to talk about themselves. It may be because they are not interested in the other person. They may be overconfident in their own knowledge and assume they know the answers. Another reason is perhaps they worry that they'll seem pushy or rude. But I think the most common reason that people don't ask enough questions is because they just don't understand how beneficial to relationships and businesses good questioning can be.

Remember that not all questions are created equal. Earlier, I mentioned the "How are you doing?" question that is not really a question at all. That falls super low on the quality-question-rating system. At the very top are follow-up questions.

Follow-up questions are questions that you ask to clarify or explore further what your conversation partner has been talking about. These are top-quality questions because they show that you are listening, interested in what the other person is saying, and want to know more. Follow-up questions take the conversation deeper and allow for more connection to build your relationship.

Listening

Hand in hand with asking questions comes listening.

There are two types of listening: active and passive. Passive listening is basically just hearing. It is listening without reacting, allowing someone to speak without interrupting. It is one-way communication where the listener doesn't give feedback or ask questions.

Active listening on the other hand includes responses that show the listener understands what the person is trying to say. This listening style shows that you've been listening, not just hearing. It shows that you genuinely understand what the other person is trying to say.

Active listening creates an environment that allows the sharer to go deeper. It encourages a connection of trust and respect. It is the foundation needed to understand the needs of customers and build strong relationships.

Reciprocity in Business Allows Others to Experience How Much You Care

Reciprocity, the giving and receiving of things and ideas among business associates, is important because it creates a sense of mutual trust and respect. By giving and receiving mutual benefits in a business relationship, associates can establish a level of cooperation that can help them navigate difficult situations and overcome challenges. Additionally, reciprocity can lead to stronger and more sustainable business relationships.

Being willing to give and receive with your fellow workers helps to foster a more collaborative and productive working environment within a business. By sharing resources and knowledge, associates can reduce costs and increase productivity, allowing them to work more efficiently and effectively. It can also help to build a sense of community and shared purpose among associates.

Reciprocity is important in business because it helps to maintain a positive reputation. Businesses and business owners that engage in reciprocity are viewed as trustworthy and reliable, which can help to attract new customers and associates.

Making Others Feel Important

In the same way that reciprocity is important in business, making others feel important is also crucial for building and maintaining positive and productive relationships with colleagues, clients, and partners. It can help improve communication, increase trust and collaboration, and boost overall productivity and success.

One way to make others feel important in business is to give them the opportunity to share their ideas and opinions. This means creating an environment where people feel comfortable speaking up and actively seeking input and feedback from team members and clients. Fostering a workplace atmosphere where others are encouraged for speaking up is essential.

Another way to make others feel important in business is to recognize and acknowledge their contributions. This can be done through verbal praise, written feedback, or bonuses and promotions. It also means giving credit where credit is due, and making sure that everyone is aware of the contributions made by their colleagues.

Being responsive to others' needs is also an important way to make coworkers, employees, and clients feel important in business. This is shown when you are prompt in answering emails, phone calls, and messages, and are willing to go the extra mile to help others.

Most importantly, showing genuine interest and care in others' personal and professional well-being is extremely important. This means being empathetic and understanding when someone is going through a difficult time and offering support.

This also includes being aware of and sensitive to cultural differences and individual needs.

Making others feel important in business is necessary for building and maintaining positive and productive relationships. It involves giving people the opportunity to share their ideas, recognizing and acknowledging their contributions, being responsive and attentive, showing genuine interest and care, and being culturally sensitive.

Final Thoughts

When I first started exploring this subject, I couldn't tell you exactly how I connected with people. I found that it came naturally to me so I didn't need to try hard or analyze what I was doing or how I did it. I just did it.

Some people are like me. Connecting with others comes easily and they genuinely like people and find them interesting. But some people will have to work on it. They will need to practice, work on their listening and question skills, and be deliberate about finding something to connect with people about.

It is important to remember the connections and conversations, but don't forget that body language will also show your interest level. There are some simple ways to sit, lean, stand, and look that will reinforce that you are interested in the person and care about what they say.

The number one thing you need to do is smile. You absolutely must smile. A smile is a great way to show you are interested in the other person and are enjoying talking to them.

Robin Dreeke was head of the FBI's Behavioral Analysis Program and studied interpersonal relations for over 30 years. He's an expert on how to connect with people and gives very practical advice.

"Keep that chin angle down so it doesn't appear like you're looking down your nose at anyone. And if you can show a little bit of a head tilt, that's always wonderful.

"You don't want to give a full frontal, full body display. That could be very offensive to someone. Give a little bit of an angle.

"So I always want to make sure that I'm showing good, open, comfortable non-verbal behaviors. I just try to use high eyebrow elevations. Basically, anything going up and elevating is very open and comforting. Anything that is compressing: lip compression, eyebrow compression, where you're squishing down, that's conveying stress."

For some people, listening and connecting will be harder than for others. But know that it is possible to grow this skill with practice. You can learn to make others feel important and valued and build relationships that last. It is the key to client-based businesses.

Questions to Ask Yourself:

1. Why is gratitude for others so important?

2. How is it possible to spend your energy focusing on the needs of others, especially in business?

3. What will you learn by listening and asking questions rather than exchanging information?

4. What are some questions you can ask customers, friends, or acquaintances to build your relationships with each person?

5. What can you do to make sure others feel important at your business?

6. What can you do physically to let others know you are interested in what they are saying?

7

KEEP PERSPECTIVE WHILE NAVIGATING CHAOS AND CHALLENGES

Everybody encounters challenges, whether it is growing up in poverty, losing a loved one, being cheated by a partner, losing a job, a business going under, being passed up for a promotion, or being sued. The question is not if you are going to have a challenge but how you will handle the inevitable hardship.

Challenges can lead to growth if you respond to them well. If you don't, they can lead to hurt and trauma.

Personal challenges can be anything from relationship problems to health issues, and they can have a significant impact on one's life. However, it is important to approach these challenges with a positive attitude. Instead of dwelling on the problem, it is important to focus on doing what you can and reaching out to others for help.

Professional challenges can come in the form of difficult coworkers or challenging circumstances. These types of challenges can be just as impactful as personal challenges, and they can also be just as difficult to overcome. However, with the right mindset, professional challenges can be a valuable opportunity to grow and develop professionally. By taking ownership of each situation you can turn the hardships into learning opportunities.

Reach out to friends if it's personal or experts if it's professional. Talking about your challenges can help you find new solutions. Instead of worrying about things you can't control, focus your energy on things that you can control. This will help you feel more empowered and less overwhelmed.

Responding to challenges is not always easy, but by focusing on finding a solution, maintaining a positive attitude, and seeing challenges as an opportunity to grow, you can overcome even the toughest of difficulties.

Keep Perspective in the Midst of Challenges

One of the key components to successfully responding to challenges is maintaining perspective. The situation you're dealing with, as difficult as it may be, is only temporary. Focus on the things in your life that you are grateful for, even if they seem small.

Let's face it, things don't always go according to plan and we're bound to encounter a few bumps along the way. It's how we handle these challenges that really define us as employees, business owners, and leaders.

Keeping perspective about the situation and the bigger picture is the most important way to get through the rough patch. Trust me, it's not rocket science, it's just about keeping a level head and a positive attitude. It is also very important to remember in the midst of chaos and challenges to not let emotions take over. Staying calm allows you to think clearly and make better decisions.

When faced with multiple challenges, it's important to prioritize which issues need to be addressed first or identify the steps that come first. This allows you to focus on the most pressing matters and ensure that they are resolved as quickly as possible.

In times of chaos, clear and effective communication is key. Make sure that everyone on your team is informed and aware of what's going on, and that they understand their roles and responsibilities.

Despite chaos and challenges, it's important to stay focused on your overall business goals. Looking past the present problems can help you stay motivated and on track. This does not mean ignoring the problem. It is important to work to overcome the present issue and learn what to do and not to do in the future to avoid it happening again.

By prioritizing, communicating effectively, being adaptable, and staying focused on your objectives, you can increase your chances of navigating through the challenges successfully and reaching your business goals.

Sometimes Closed Doors Are Exactly What We Need

Losing the opportunity that I had worked toward for years at Blue Shield, becoming vice president of sales, was extremely hard at the time. Not only did I feel betrayed, but I questioned everything, including my career choice. I'm sure Carla heard a few choice things that I had to say about the company.

Only a few years later, however, I felt completely different. In fact, I came to realize that being passed up for the position was the best thing they could have done for me. It forced me onto the path that eventually led me to business ownership and self-storage. Honestly, I shudder a little when I think about what my and my family's life would look like now if I had gotten that promotion. I know that we would not be who we are today.

Lost opportunities can feel like the end of the world at the time, but they can also be a good thing. It may be hard to see the silver lining when an opportunity slips through your fingers, but trust me, it's there. Lost opportunities and closed doors can actually be a positive thing.

When an opportunity is lost, it can be a real disappointment. But, instead of dwelling on what could have been, reflect on why the opportunity was lost and what you can do differently next time. This can help you identify areas for improvement and ultimately lead to personal growth.

Closed doors can also lead to finding a better opportunity. In my situation, it led me to look for another insurance company. Without losing the opportunity at Blue Shield, I never would have found Johnson and Higgins and had an opportunity to open and run my own office in Boise, Idaho.

Lost opportunities can help to clarify priorities.

It can be a wake-up call and help you realize what is truly important to you and what you want to focus on. This can help you make better decisions in the future and prioritize what is most important to you and your family.

Closed doors and lost opportunities can teach you to appreciate what you have. When an opportunity is lost, it can be easy to focus on what you don't have. It's important to remember to be grateful for what you do have, appreciate the good things in your life, and not take them for granted.

Losing an opportunity can be difficult, but it can also help us to build resilience. It teaches us to handle failure and to bounce back from it. We learn to be persistent and to not give up.

Lost opportunities offer a new opportunity to build a stronger network and relationships by reaching out to others and seeking guidance and support. By consulting others, you can gain valuable insights and advice that can help open new doors in the future.

Next time an opportunity falls through, try to see the silver lining and use it as an opportunity to grow and learn. It can also be an opportunity to reassess goals and redirect efforts toward something more suitable and fulfilling.

When You Learn From a Challenge, You Walk Away a Better Person

Challenges in life and business are unavoidable. However, learning from a challenge can be a valuable and rewarding experience. When we encounter a challenge, it forces us to think critically and creatively, to come up with new solutions, and to develop new skills. In essence, when you can walk away from a challenge you have overcome, you walk away a better person.

Not everyone does this. Some people allow the problem to get the better of them and can become bitter, cynical, or withdrawn.

Learning from a challenge requires a growth mindset, a willingness to learn and try new things, and the ability to reflect and receive feedback. Taking a proactive approach by seeking out new learning opportunities and reading up on relevant information can help you gain new knowledge and skills that can help overcome future challenges. Reflect on what you have learned from the experience and how you can apply it to future challenges.

Remember that failure is not an end, it's an opportunity to improve. This is not a cliché but something you really can embrace in life and business.

Handling Relationships Gone Bad in Business

I am thankful that I have only had a few relationships go bad in business. Each time was hard but I found that there are a few steps to help all parties get through it and either resolve the issue and move forward or walk away and move on.

It's important to stay calm and professional, even if the other party is upset or angry. Emotions can run high in these situations but by maintaining a levelheaded demeanor you'll be better equipped to address the issue at hand.

Next, make sure you're actively listening to the other party. Allow them to express their concerns and frustrations fully and show them that you're listening by summarizing what they've said and asking follow-up questions. This will help you understand their perspective and give you insight into how to address the issue.

If you or your company is at fault in the situation, it's important to take responsibility for your actions and apologize. Owning up to your mistakes will show the other party that you're willing to make amends.

Once you've both expressed your concerns, try to find common ground. Look for areas where both parties can agree and work toward finding a solution that benefits everyone. It's important to remember that finding a compromise may not be easy but it's important to try.

Communication is key in any relationship, and that's especially true when things have gone bad. Keep the lines of communication open and check in on the progress of the resolution. It is also important to keep a record of all communication. This will ensure that everyone is on the same page and working toward the same goal.

Finally, if you're unable to resolve the issue on your own, don't be afraid to seek help. A mediator or another leader may be able to offer a fresh perspective and help you find a solution.

It's important to remember that relationships, especially in business, can be complex, and not always easy to maintain. But with open communication, active listening, and a willingness to compromise, you can work through the tough times and come out on the other side with a stronger relationship.

If compromise is not an option or if the issue is a moral one (theft, dishonesty, etc.), keeping on the path to resolving the situation means remaining calm, involving the authorities if needed, and taking steps to not repeat the situation in the future.

Do what you need to do. Let the employee go. Dissolve the partnership. Refuse to use the vendor in the future. Rewrite and improve the contract. There are ways that you can avoid the situation in the future. Running a smooth business means working through conflict with your partners, employees, and clients, but doing so in a professional manner will ensure a good reputation.

Final Thoughts

If you want to avoid conflict and challenges in life, don't own a business or work as an employee. In fact, you will need to not have any family or friends, interact with anyone or have any needs yourself. Challenges and chaos are a part of life. Learning to navigate them is part of growing and becoming a better person. Don't let them discourage you. The more you overcome, the more you can overcome.

One of the factors that you always need to consider when you experience challenges is what your role in them has been. If you find that you are experiencing the same kind of problems again and again, ask yourself what the common factor is. Be honest with yourself and ask if it's you.

So many people play the blame game. They look for what the problem is without ever considering that it could be them. Many people have a victim mentality. They refuse to take responsibility for any problem or challenge.

Let me tell you honestly, victims can't lead. Victims cannot become good bosses, managers, or business owners. Only when we take responsibility for ourselves, our job, our department, or our business can we make the right decisions and steer the ship to success.

Taking responsibility is a commitment to own your life, to self-leadership, growth and freedom.

– Christopher Avery

Questions to Ask Yourself:

1. How should I handle challenges?

2. How do I know if a problem is too big for me to handle alone?

3. What is a healthy mindset about obstacles and problems in business and life?

4. How do I survive relationships gone bad in business?

5. What are some potential challenges that may arise in my particular business?

6. What are some personal issues that I can work on strengthening?

8

RUN YOUR BUSINESS (AND LIFE) WITH INTEGRITY

My cell phone rang as I was getting ready for bed. I tried not to take work calls after business hours, but when I checked who was calling, I got a sinking feeling. It was Rick, my IT guy. I had asked him to check one of my agent's work emails. I had heard a disturbing rumor that Devon was planning on leaving Western Benefit Solutions, my company, and moving to another. That was all good and fine, but the rumor had included him poaching clients illegally.

As I answered the phone, I braced myself for bad news. Rick wouldn't call this late with anything but bad news.

"Rick, what's up?" I skipped the pleasantries. I knew he would want to get right into it.

"Ron, I'm afraid I found some disturbing emails from Devon. He *has* been giving our client information to another insurance agency. He's sent them not only a ton of our client's names and contacts, but the worst part is that Devon sent them the policy and premium information for The Johnson Group, Eagle Eye Properties, and Montano.

"Oh, that's bad." They were three of the largest clients that Devon handled. This was worse than I had imagined.

I thanked Rick after telling him to document the emails. I had things to do.

The next morning I arrived at work earlier than normal. I hadn't been able to sleep well all night thinking about his betrayal not just for the company but for me personally. I thought he was a friend. In fact, Carla and I had just taken him and his wife to dinner last month.

Devon didn't usually arrive until 9 a.m. and I wanted to be ready and prepared to send him packing.

I let my leadership team know what was going on. Then I contacted our lawyer. After getting the instructions for how to handle Devon's termination, including what to say, I asked our two largest, most intimidating managers to be available to escort Devon out once I talked to him.

Everything was ready when he came in at 9:23 a.m. After he took his jacket off and before he booted up his computer, I knocked on his office door.

"Devon."

"Morning Ron. How's it going? It's a beautiful day outside!" His greeting was overly bright and maybe a bit nervous.

I dove right in, "Devon, we checked your email and found that you've been giving our client information to another insurance agency." I let the silence hang.

"Wha . . .

"Nnnnn . . .

"I . . .

"Stop." I interrupted. "Grab your jacket and car keys and leave. Right. Now. We will box up anything that is yours and send it to your house. You will also be hearing from our lawyers."

As he looked at me with wide eyes and a flushed face, I stepped back so my two large managers could step in.

That was the beginning of a long, hard process where we ended up losing two of those three large clients and going to court over his blatant non-compete breach.

But the most interesting thing about the whole situation is that Devon only worked for them for about a year. He lost his good job with us, lost his integrity by stealing our clients and information, and then started working for a company without integrity. And then they let him go after establishing "his" clients with their company.

What goes around, comes around.

There are many businesses that don't keep their word, use deceptive marketing, treat their people and employees badly, and offer shoddy services. And those companies usually don't thrive.

On the other hand, the sky is the limit for businesses with a stellar reputation, honest owners and employees, and a good business model.

Your Reputation in Life and Business Is the Most Important Way to Advertise

You know what they say: "Your reputation is everything." And when it comes to life and business, that statement couldn't be truer. Your reputation is like a personal billboard, advertising who you are and what you stand for to everyone around you.

Think about it, when you hear a friend or colleague talk about someone they know. What do they usually say? "Oh, they're really reliable" or "They always deliver on time." Those are examples of a good reputation, and it's something that can really set you apart in life and business.

Having a good reputation can open doors for you in life and business that you never thought possible. People are more likely to trust and work with someone who has a good reputation. It's like a seal of approval from the community, and it can make the difference in getting that big contract or landing that dream job.

But it's not just about what others think of you. Having a good reputation can also be beneficial to your own personal growth. When you have a good reputation, you'll be more inclined to take on new challenges and push yourself to be the best you can be.

The best way to build and maintain a good reputation is by being consistent and reliable. Be true to your word, deliver on your promises, and always go above and beyond to help others. It's important to be honest and transparent in all your actions and decisions and to be willing to admit and correct your mistakes.

Another key component to building and maintaining a good reputation is by being actively engaged in your community. Whether it's volunteering, sponsoring nonprofits in the community, or mentoring young people, community involvement shows that you care about the people around you and are willing to give back.

In the end, your reputation is the sum of all your actions and decisions, and it's a reflection of who you are as a person. By being upright and honorable, consistent and reliable, and actively engaged in your community, you can build a reputation that will serve you well in life and business.

A Good Reputation Grows Your Business

When it comes to growing your business, word-of-mouth referrals are one of the most powerful tools at your disposal. And a big part of getting those referrals is having a good reputation.

When someone has had a great experience with a business or individual, they're more likely to tell their friends and family about it. And that's where the power of referrals comes in. People are more likely to trust a recommendation from someone they know, rather than a stranger or an advertisement.

And it's not just about getting new customers—having a good reputation also leads to repeat business. When someone has had a positive experience with your business, they're more likely to come back.

But how do you build and maintain a good reputation in business? One of the most important things is to provide excellent customer service. Being able to get a live person on the phone, handling problems promptly, and being able to meet customers' needs are ways to set your business apart from the competition.

When you go above and beyond to help your customers, they're more likely to remember you and recommend you to others.

Another key component is to be transparent and honest in all your actions and decisions, especially financially. Honesty is an important value that will help you build trust with your customers.

Finally, always be willing to listen and take feedback from your customers. When you take the time to listen to your customers and make improvements based on their feedback, you show that you value their input and care about their satisfaction.

In short, having a good reputation in business can be the key to getting more referrals and growing your business. By providing excellent customer service, being transparent and honest, and taking feedback, you can establish a reputation that will serve you well in the long run.

How to Make a Big Difference

When it comes to making a difference in people's lives, there are a few key things that can really make a big impact: offering education, providing quality services, putting in hard work, and having clear and honest communication.

One of the ways that I built my insurance business was by offering free insurance education to clients and even other insurance agents. Semi-annually, I rented out a conference room, provide drinks and snacks, and offer free admission to the seminar to clients and insurance agents.

I would bring in experts to talk about the newest laws, the latest updated insurance information, and even niche issues that I knew people were dealing with. This was especially important during the national transition to the Affordable Care Act (Obamacare). Everything about insurance changed during those years and there were so many questions. For a few years, our attendance more than doubled.

These education seminars cost me a pretty penny. But they also earned me loyalty, a reputation as an expert in insurance, and a lot of gratitude. I never regretted them.

Now that I am out of insurance, I usually speak at different conferences around the country. I speak regularly at the Self-Storage Income live event held yearly in northern Idaho. I've spoken at the Self-Storage Association National Conference four times, the Inside Self-Storage National Conference twice, and various other state associations for self-storage. I talk about what is happening in the self-storage industry and how owners can increase their profits. I love it and am still passionate about education.

Offering quality services also makes a huge impact on people. Whether you're a business owner, a professional, or just someone trying to help others, providing high-quality services makes a difference. When you offer quality services, you're showing that you care about your customers or clients and that you're committed to helping them in the best way possible.

Another important factor is putting in hard work. No matter what you do, putting in the effort and dedication to do your best can influence others' lives. When you work hard, you're demonstrating that you're willing to go the extra mile and that you're committed to achieving success.

Clear and honest communication is also crucial.

Whether you're talking to customers, clients, or team members, being able to communicate effectively and honestly can make a huge difference. When you're clear and upfront about your expectations, goals, and plans, it can help people understand what you're trying to achieve and how they can help. Honest communication also builds trust and creates a positive environment for everyone.

All these elements together can help build a strong and reliable reputation, which is vital for any individual or business. When people know they can depend on you to provide quality services and that you have their best interests in mind, they will naturally recommend you to others.

On the other hand, providing poor services, lack of effort, and poor communication can have the opposite effect. It can lead to negative reviews, loss of customers, and a damaged reputation, which can take years to overcome.

It's important to remember that building a good reputation takes time, but it can be lost quickly. So, it's essential to consistently deliver quality services, put in hard work and effort, and practice clear and honest communication.

In addition to that, it's important to be willing to learn and improve. No one is perfect, and there will always be room for improvement. Being open to feedback and constructive criticism can help you identify areas where you can improve and make a bigger difference.

In the end, the small things matter. The extra effort you put in to make sure a customer is satisfied, taking the time to explain something in more detail, or going out of your way to help someone can make a big difference in people's lives.

Equal Respectability in Your Business and Personal Life Brings Success

One thing I know for sure about respectability is that you can't be honest and respectable in your business and not in your personal life. And the opposite is true. You can't be a shark at work and amazing and gracious out of the office. Life is not separated like that (or at least shouldn't be). When you do business well, your clients become your friends and your friends and family become your clients.

On the business side of things, when you treat your employees, customers, and clients with respect, they'll feel valued and appreciated. And when people feel valued and appreciated, they tend to not only work harder and be more loyal to you but also become friends.

But it's not just about treating others with respect in the professional realm, it's important to do the same in your personal life as well. When you treat your friends, family, and significant other with respect, they'll feel more valued and appreciated. Plus, when you treat people with respect, it's more likely that they'll reciprocate. And when people respect you, they're more likely to trust you and want to do business with you. It's a win-win situation.

You Can't Separate Friends From Business Associates

When it comes to business, some people get caught up in the idea of keeping your personal and professional lives separate. But not only is that not possible it's also not a good idea. If you run your business with integrity and honesty, putting clients first, there is no reason to keep your friendships separate from your business associates. In fact, when your business has an excellent reputation, your business associates will want to become your friends.

Why would you want to separate friends from business associates? It's like trying to separate peanut butter from jelly—it just doesn't make sense. Keeping friends and business associates separate is missing out on the true magic of networking and building relationships.

Everyone Is Watching You (Including Your Kids)

Integrity is a vital aspect of both personal and professional life, and it's something that everyone, including your kids, is paying attention to. Your actions and decisions, big or small, reflect on the kind of person you are and the kind of example you set for those around you.

One of the key aspects of integrity is honesty. Being truthful and transparent in your actions and words is crucial for building trust and respect among those around you. It's not just about avoiding dishonesty, it's also about being willing to admit when you've made a mistake and take responsibility for it.

Integrity also encompasses consistency. Being true to your values and principles, regardless of the situation, is a fundamental aspect of integrity. It's not just about being a good person when things are going well, it's also about standing up for what's right when faced with adversity.

Another important aspect of integrity is fairness. Treating others with respect and giving them a fair chance, regardless of their background or circumstances, is crucial for building strong relationships and fostering a positive environment.

Integrity also involves being reliable and dependable. Following through on your commitments and being accountable for your actions is essential for building trust and respect among those around you.

By striving to act with integrity, you not only set a good example for those around you, but you also build trust, respect, and strong relationships. Remember, integrity is not something you can turn on and off. It's a way of living.

Final Thoughts

Integrity is a big deal to me. It was one of the things I taught my kids. I made sure to act the same behind closed doors in my house as I did at the office, at church, and on vacation.

If you have integrity, nothing else matters.
If you don't have integrity, nothing else matters.

—Harvey Mackay

Integrity is not something that you decide to start one day. It takes courage, perseverance, effort, and honesty. It is about determining to do what you say you will do with no excuses. It is about being honest about mistakes and taking responsibility to correct them. It is even about saying no to opportunities because of a previous commitment you made.

Integrity does not always look the same. But it is about choosing to do the "right" thing no matter what.

I had a partner once who stopped contributing to our business. He would rarely come into the office and stopped dealing with any of the business issues. Thankfully, we had started our partnership with an agreement that included how to dissolve the partnership if one or both of us wished.

I felt like the right thing to do for my family and the business was to buy him out. The process was long, hard, and emotional. The easier thing to do would have been to keep going the way things had been going. But I knew that ending it and paying him what we had agreed to contractually was the right thing.

Acting with integrity is not easy but it is worth it. Your family, your business, and your community will benefit.

Questions to Ask Yourself:

1. How can my business stand out from the crowd?

2. What principles should I follow for getting and keeping clients/customers?

3. What are the most important moral issues to me? (Honesty, hard work, etc.)

4. Is there any integrity issues I need to work on personally?

5. What kind of reputation do I want my business to have?

6. How can I encourage word-of-mouth referrals?

9

KEEP YOUR EYES WIDE OPEN FOR OPPORTUNITY

I have learned a very sneaky truth over my years of business both in the insurance world and in self-storage. Opportunity often comes looking like something else entirely.

Many people have been surprised when an opportunity arose in an unexpected place.

It could look like a friend with skills, vision, and passion in an area that interests you. It could look like a job that you accepted out of desperation because you needed to pay the rent and eat. It could look like your grandmother needing help with her yard and sparking a business idea. It could even look like a friendship built from a painting job that turns into an entirely different career.

I know a guy who did what he had to do to pay the bills when he was young, newly married, and had small mouths to feed.

He worked as a building painter. One of his painting jobs was a music recording studio in Boise, Idaho. He became friends with the owner and they connected over music. It turns out that the owner needed a person to record the music bands and was willing to train the painter as a recording engineer. That began the painter's new career that eventually, over 15 years, led to working on sound for films and TV and now, he works for Disney recording actors' voices.

Having the eyes to see hidden opportunities is about having an entrepreneurial mindset and being willing when the opportunity is right. It's not about jumping at every opportunity. It's about evaluating and critically thinking about the pros and cons, the how to and how not to, and the outcome. It's also about evaluating how that opportunity might change your life, for better or worse.

Take Every Opportunity to Build Relationships/Friendships

The vast majority of opportunities come from relationships. Even after graduating from college, connections with professors and guidance counselors often open opportunities for good jobs. Even when you're established in a solid business, it's important to remember that every relationship is a good opportunity. Whether you're at a networking event, a company retreat, or just grabbing lunch with a colleague, you never know when a new connection may lead to something more.

One of the best ways to build relationships and friendships in business is to simply be yourself. Don't be afraid to let your personality shine through and let people get to know the real you. After all, people do business with people they like and trust.

Another great way to build relationships and friendships in business is to be generous with your time and expertise. Whether it's offering to help a colleague with a project or providing valuable advice to a client, going above and beyond to be helpful can go a long way in building strong connections.

When building relationships, don't be afraid to get a little creative. You can never go wrong with a thoughtful gesture or a personal touch. For example, you can send a handwritten note, a small gift, or even a meme that you think they would enjoy. It'll show that you're paying attention and that you care.

It's also important to remember that building relationships and friendships in business is not a one-way street. It's important to give and take.

Don't be afraid to laugh at yourself. This is something that I am quite good at. Being able to laugh at yourself and not take yourself too seriously can go a long way in building relationships and friendships. It shows that you're human and easygoing.

Building relationships and friendships in business is about taking advantage of every opportunity, being yourself, being generous, being a good listener, getting creative, being supportive, and not taking yourself too seriously. Just remember, building relationships is like planting a garden: it takes time and effort, but it will bear fruit.

Sometimes Opportunity Comes Disguised in the Coat of Another Career

Over the decades of my insurance career, I had opportunities to pivot in my career. I started out with medical and life insurance, then pivoted to small business insurance. A few years later, I began working for Blue Shield and eventually moved to their headquarters and ran their sales department.

My next pivot in insurance was to work for Johnson and Higgins and then start my own office in Boise, Idaho. After that ended, I started an insurance company called Western Benefit Solutions (WBS).

My career took a completely different turn when I sold WBS and started a self-storage investment company with one of my sons and my son-in-law. And until then, I never would have believed I'd be where I am now.

The opportunity came disguised in the coat of an entirely different career. And I am so happy it did.

Just like for me, opportunities can come in many forms, whether it's a job offer, a volunteer gig, or even a random conversation with someone. It's important to be looking and if the opportunity seems right, take a chance, because you never know where it might lead.

It's also important to remember that opportunities can come at any stage of your career. Whether you're just starting out, or you've been in the same job for 20 years, it's never too late to try something new. Sometimes, the best opportunities come from stepping out of your comfort zone and doing something different.

Occasionally, an opportunity can feel like you're taking a step back, but sometimes you have to be willing to take a step back to take two steps forward. Sometimes, taking a step back in your career can lead to a more fulfilling and successful future.

Networking is also an important aspect of finding opportunities. It's a good idea to expand your professional network as much as possible. This means attending industry events, joining professional organizations, or even reaching out to people in your field to ask for advice.

Remember, opportunities can come in many forms, and it's never too late to try something new. Keep your eyes and ears open, expand your professional network, and don't be afraid to take a step back to take two steps forward.

Successful People Are Not Foolish—They Are Careful but Willing

Successful people understand that taking risks is an important part of achieving success, but they also know that it's important to be strategic and thoughtful about the risks they take.

For example, a successful entrepreneur might carefully research a new business venture before investing their time and money into it. They might also seek advice from experienced mentors or industry experts to help them make informed decisions.

Similarly, a successful investor might carefully research a stock before buying shares. They might also diversify their portfolio to minimize risk.

Being careful doesn't mean being afraid of taking risks. Successful people are willing to take calculated risks because they understand that without taking risks, it's impossible to achieve great success.

When AJ, Sam, and I started Bitterroot Holdings, our self-storage investment company, we spent months carefully planning everything from the ground up. We each brought different strengths to the table and our collaboration created a strong business foundation.

We knew that starting a business is always a risk, but if we were careful, we could minimize those risks.

And our planning paid off. Bitterroot Holdings has been a huge success.

We did make mistakes along the way, but we were still successful because we understood that failure is a natural part of the learning process. We knew it was important to learn from past mistakes in order to make better decisions in the future.

Having a clear vision of what we wanted to achieve helped us set specific, measurable, and achievable goals to get there.

Over the years, as an opportunity came up, I made sure to evaluate each opportunity objectively instead of jumping into every one. If I thought it was a good fit, I would take a step forward and reevaluate. If that process led me through the door, I knew it was for me.

Find Opportunities That Meet Your Criteria, but Don't Change Your Criteria to Meet an Opportunity

It's important to remember that when looking for opportunities, whether it's in your field of interest or not, stick to your own criteria and don't change them to fit a specific opportunity. And in order to do that, you need to know what your criteria is.

If you're looking for a job and you have certain requirements such as a certain salary range, location, or type of work, it's important to not lower your standards just to take a job that doesn't meet those criteria. The same goes for starting a business or investing in a company. It's important to do your research and make sure that the opportunity aligns with your values and goals.

Changing your criteria to fit an opportunity can lead to dissatisfaction and regret in the long run. Remember that it's okay to walk away from an opportunity that doesn't align with your values and goal.

On the other hand, if you keep your criteria in mind and look for opportunities that meet them, you're more likely to find something that you'll be happy with in the long run.

Don't Be Limited by Lack of Knowledge

Many people believe that they can't pursue a certain opportunity or career path because they don't have enough experience or knowledge in that field. But it's important to remember that everyone has to start somewhere and you can always learn and grow.

If you're interested in starting a business but don't have any experience in entrepreneurship, you can take classes, read books, or mentor with someone who has experience. Similarly, if you're interested in a career change but don't have the necessary skills or qualifications, you can take courses or get certified in that field. Online courses and certifications are a great way to gain knowledge and skills in the specific field, and they are also more accessible and affordable than ever.

Don't be afraid to start small. It is usually wise to start with small projects or jobs to gain experience and knowledge before taking on bigger responsibilities. It's better to start small, learn as you go, and gradually increase your responsibilities, rather than taking on too much too soon and getting overwhelmed.

It's also important to remember that a lack of knowledge or experience doesn't mean that you can't contribute value or make a difference. Sometimes, new perspectives and fresh ideas can be just as valuable as years of experience. Many times, experienced people are stuck in their ways, and new ideas can be the breath of fresh air that a company or project needs.

As I mentioned earlier in the book, attending industry events, joining professional organizations, or even reaching out to people in your desired field for advice and guidance will build your knowledge.

And remember, another way to gain knowledge and experience is through internships. This is a great way to gain hands-on experience in a field you are interested in, and to learn from people who have been working in the field for a while. You will end that time knowing for sure if you want to continue pursuing that field.

As I've said before, failure is a part of the learning process. Don't be discouraged if you face setbacks or obstacles—instead, use them as opportunities to learn and grow. And don't be afraid to ask questions. If you don't know something, that's okay! It's always better to ask and learn, rather than pretending to know something you don't and mess up.

Don't be afraid to take risks and to step out of your comfort zone.

Sometimes the greatest opportunities come from taking a chance and trying something new. The most successful people don't let lack of knowledge or inexperience stop them from pursuing opportunities. With the right attitude and willingness to learn, the opportunities are endless.

Don't Be Limited by Geography

We live in a new day and age. Many things changed during the COVID pandemic and one of the major ones was remote work. Most companies that stayed afloat during that hard time had to pivot to remote work. And a good majority still offer it today. This has opened up the opportunity to work for companies in other states and even in other countries.

With the continued advancements in technology and the internet, there are even more opportunities that can be done remotely or from anywhere in the world.

If you're looking for a job, there are many companies that offer remote positions or allow employees to work from home. This means that you can apply for jobs all over the country, or even internationally, without having to move or uproot your family.

Similarly, if you're starting a business or investing in a company, you can do so from anywhere in the world. With the power of the internet, you can reach a global market and have customers or clients from all over the world.

There are many online platforms, such as freelance marketplaces, that allow you to offer your services or skills to a global audience. This means that you can earn money from wherever you are, as long as you have an internet connection.

Don't limit yourself to just the opportunities available in your immediate area. Think about exploring opportunities all over the world and taking advantage of the power of the internet to expand your reach and find new opportunities.

Cautions

It's important to always be on the lookout for business and growth opportunities, but it's equally important to be cautious and use good judgment. You should always be skeptical of opportunities that seem too good to be true. These types of opportunities often come with hidden catches or risks and can end up costing you more in the long run.

Critical thinking, research, advice from experts, and avoiding getting emotionally invested are essential when considering any opportunity, regardless of how attractive it may seem at first glance. This includes thoroughly evaluating the potential return on investment, as well as any risks or downsides associated with the opportunity.

Do Your Own Research and Then Get Advice

When it comes to identifying and evaluating opportunities, it's important to do your own research. Look into the opportunity yourself and completely evaluate both the potential return on investment, as well as all drawbacks and risks. By doing your own research first, you'll be better equipped to ask informed questions and make the right decision for you.

Be curious and ask questions! Understand all sides of the opportunity and its potential impact on your business. Gather all the information you can and make sure you are clear on what is required to make the opportunity successful.

After you have answered every question you can, seek advice from a variety of sources. This includes talking to industry experts, consulting with other business owners, and seeking the advice of a financial adviser or mentor. Each person may have a unique perspective or insight that can help you to make a more informed decision.

Remember, not all advice is created equal, and it's important to seek the advice of people who have relevant experience and expertise.

Beware of Tunnel Vision (Because You Are Too Excited)

Tunnel vision can happen when you become so focused on a particular opportunity that you fail to consider other options or potential risks. This can be particularly dangerous when you are excited about a new opportunity, as it can cloud your judgment and lead you to make impulsive or ill-informed decisions.

To avoid the pitfalls of tunnel vision, it's important to take a step back and consider the bigger picture. This includes looking at the opportunity from different angles and evaluating it in the context of your overall goals and strategy. It's also important to consider the potential risks and downsides of the opportunity, as well as any other options that may be available to you.

The hardest but one of the most important things to be aware of is your own biases and assumptions. We all have a tendency to see things in a certain way, and it's important to be aware of this and to question your own assumptions. This can help you to be more objective and to avoid being swayed by personal biases or emotions.

The best way to avoid an inappropriate opportunity commitment that's inflluenced by emotion is time and evaluation. Most salespeople understand pressure, fear of missing out, and impulse tactics. When you take the time to research the opportunity and ask advice, you are guaranteed to make a smart, levelheaded decision. That doesn't mean you can't be excited about the opportunity, but being excited while keeping your eyes open about possible challenges is the best way to make decisions.

When my kids would bargain for souvenirs while on vacation, I'd always tell them, "You will get the best price possible if you are willing to walk away from the deal. And the same is true for opportunities. If you hold it in an open hand and are willing to walk away if you find it is not for you, the opportunities that work out will be the right ones for you.

Always Look for Ways to Improve Your Business With Technology/Innovation

I am grateful for technology in the self-storage industry. We have implemented quite a few things that have made our storage businesses safer and run smoother. Surprisingly, technology has also helped fill gaps in the labor shortage.

We now use smart locks, automatic gates, and digital entry codes in most of our self-storage sites. These technologies give the customer access without keys 24 hours a day, seven days a week. It also helps us monitor the site, grant or restrict access, and manage the security from anywhere.

One of the problems that self-storage facilities have been dealing with for the last few years is a labor shortage. This has been a national problem, not just in our industry, but in most service-based industries. Self-storage companies haven't been able to find committed workers to staff their facilities during the hours they are open. There have been countless times when facilities have had to lock their doors during the day because of the labor shortage. Thankfully, this does not hinder renters from accessing their units, but it does hurt the chances of gaining more customers.

After failing to hire enough workers even when offered good financial incentives, the self-storage industry has been coming up with innovative solutions to the problem. One of the solutions they have created is virtual greeters. They have installed digital screens in the entrances of storage facility office buildings.

When a customer opens the front door, it triggers a call to a live person stationed in a corporate office. Their live video image is projected onto a see-through digital screen in the facility office and can greet and interact with the customer, doing everything but walking them around the facility. The live virtual greeter can answer questions, rent units, and set up payments. It has been a huge success and allows one skilled person to cover multiple facilities.

In ours and most other industries, it's essential to stay on top of the latest technology and innovation. Keeping up with the latest developments in technology gives business owners a competitive edge, helps streamline operations, and opens up new opportunities for growth and expansion.

I also make sure I have a solid understanding of what's happening in my industry by attending conferences, joining trade organizations, and networking with other professionals.

Another way to stay current with technology is to invest in training and development for yourself and your employees. By providing your team with the skills and knowledge they need to use technology effectively, you can help them to be more productive, efficient, and motivated.

Keep in mind that technology and innovation are not limited to new software or hardware. It also includes new processes, new ways of thinking, and new business models. For example, a new way of creating a product or delivering a service can be an innovative solution.

Remember, not all new ideas will work, but don't be afraid to try something new. As long as you're prepared to learn from your mistakes and move on, experimentation is a great way to learn and grow.

Passive Income

Sometimes opportunity won't cost time, effort, or a pivot in your career. Sometimes the best opportunities will only cost a financial investment. I am talking about finding an opportunity for investments that make passive income.

Passive income is a great way to earn money without actively working for it. There are many different ways to generate passive income, and the opportunities for doing so are growing all the time.

One of the most popular ways to generate passive income is through real estate investing. This is how I started out. I looked for a long-term investment that could generate passive income while I poured my heart and soul into Western Benefit Solutions, my insurance brokerage. I researched different types of real estate investments and finally decided on self-storage facilities. It was the best fit for me.

There are many ways to create passive income through real estate. By owning commercial property, you can earn income from rent payments without having to actively manage the property. There are also REITs (real estate investment trusts), which allow you to invest in a portfolio of properties, giving you exposure to the real estate market without the need to own or manage property directly.

Another way to generate passive income is through investing in dividend-paying stocks. These stocks pay a regular dividend to shareholders, which can provide a steady stream of income without having to actively trade the stock.

You can also generate passive income by creating and selling digital products like ebooks, courses, or apps. Once created, these products can be sold over and over again, providing a steady stream of income.

Purchasing and holding onto assets like precious metals, cryptocurrencies, or collectibles that have the potential to appreciate in value over time can also be opportunities for passive income.

There are endless ways to generate passive income and as technology grows, our culture changes, and innovations advance, there will more and more ways to create passive income. However, it is important to find one that fits your interests, skills, and resources. With the right strategy, a bit of initial effort, or the right investment partner, you can create a steady stream of income that requires minimal effort on your part.

Final Thoughts

Opportunities can be found anywhere and the majority of them come from relationships and connections. However, it is important to not treat any relationship as a commodity.

Yes, we benefit from connections with people whether it is friendship, business opportunity, family growth, or knowledge. But we have something to offer relationships too.

Relationships are a two-way street. We create the deepest connections with people when we have something to give and something to receive. Relationships can bring numerous benefits to our lives, but it's important to remember that we also have something valuable to offer in return. By contributing to the relationship, we can create a sense of purpose and fulfillment, knowing that we are making a positive impact in someone else's life.

In a friendship, we can offer support and encouragement, providing a listening ear and a shoulder to lean on. In a business relationship, we can bring our skills, expertise, and passion to the table, helping to drive success and growth. In a family relationship, we can offer love, support, and guidance, helping to foster a sense of connection and belonging.

By offering something of value to others, we can strengthen our relationships and create lasting connections. When people feel appreciated and valued, they are more likely to return the favor, leading to a mutually beneficial relationship. Additionally, by giving to others, we can also develop a sense of gratitude and compassion, which can enhance our overall well-being and happiness.

Questions to Ask Yourself:

1. How can I build relationships in my industry?

2. How will I know when I am ready to invest/pivot?

3. How much of my time, money, and focus should I invest in new opportunities?

4. What are some innovations that are being developed for my industry?

5. What are some ways I can begin to generate passive income?

6. How can I become more aware of opportunities both personally and professionally?

CONCLUSION

Building a solid foundation that leads to a rewarding and lucrative career is not about ego, getting rich, or conquering the world. Having a worthwhile profession is about stability, provision, and making a difference in your family and community. And starting well in business, whether it is on your own or for someone else, will give you the head start to get there sooner and more securely.

Your choice of career is the first major decision you will make when starting out.

If you are in college and have a major, you already know what you want to do. If you aren't college oriented or are in the middle of another career and are thinking about pivoting, evaluating your future business path will be your first major step forward.

Choose wisely. Think about your strengths and weaknesses, your interests and talents, and your qualifications and investment abilities. Choose a career that will go the long haul, has a good return on investment, and has the ability to grow and scale. Having the right mindset about business will help you evaluate jobs, careers, and business opportunities.

Being always willing to learn means acknowledging that you don't know it all yet. A lifelong learner is always working to increase their skills and knowledge and is looking for opportunities to connect with experts in the fields they have chosen. Learning increases curiosity which leads to excitement about possibilities. When you keep learning, you keep growing, and you encourage growth in your business, company, and industry.

Make it a point to expand your skills, knowledge, and ideas. In nature, there is no such thing as remaining the same. Nature, like humans, is either growing or dying. In the same ways, your knowledge and skills are either growing or dying. Nurture them. Grow them.

Balancing life and work is an important skill. Giving too much time and effort to one or the other creates stress and decreases satisfaction and joy. Part of that balance is focusing on your community. Finding ways to contribute with finances or time can bring that sense of balance. And balancing life with family is not the only option. Friends can become family and part of your close community.

Choose to not focus all your energy on work or all on your home life. Hobbies, relaxing, fun, and time with family and friends are important and should help balance a full work schedule. On the other hand, if you find yourself giving too much time and attention to fun and entertainment, they should be balanced with work and career pursuits. Maturity and responsibility create balance.

Another part of living in a balanced way is being in control of your finances. Going through life with your eyes closed to your income and spending brings stress, especially when emergencies happen. Living paycheck to paycheck brings stress and fear.

Live differently so you can choose a different life. Budget your income. Make sure there is enough to put aside for emergencies and then invest for the future. When your finances stop controlling you, life and future possibilities change.

Understanding the practical aspects of business, like business types, cash flow, getting professionals to help, business plans, marketing, and insurance is a huge part of starting well in business. A foundation of how a business solidifies, runs, and grows will help you not only with your own business but also as an employee. If you find yourself lacking, reach out to people for help. Eventually, you will be able to help others like you were helped.

Businesses are people-based—even factories, accounting firms, or IT companies. People make up the clients, the employees, and the management. Knowing how to grow relationships and connect with people will help you do business well. Connecting and growing relationships will give you a head start when looking for clients, hiring employees, and interacting with coworkers.

Make people feel important. Learn to listen and ask questions. The process of getting to know people is gratifying and creates connections not just in your personal life, but in business.

Life is not always smooth and easy. Chaos and challenges will come both in your personal life as well as in your business. How you navigate them is up to you. Staying levelheaded, asking for help, and learning from your mistakes are all ways to get through the issue as quickly as possible. If you can keep a good perspective about the challenge, you will come out a better person, able to navigate future challenges more smoothly.

Keep perspective about the challenges you are facing. Remember that they are opportunities for growth, and by approaching them with the right attitude, you can overcome them and come out stronger.

Running your business with integrity will set your business apart from the competition. That means operating in a transparent and honest manner and treating customers, employees, and partners with respect and fairness. By having integrity in all aspects of your business, you can create a strong business with a good reputation.

Be honest. Do what you say you'll do. Treat others fairly. Provide quality products and services. Be consistent. Integrity creates a strong reputation and ensures repeat customers and referrals.

Listen with curiosity.

Speak with honesty.

Act with integrity.

—Roy T. Bennett

As we go through life, we will find personal and professional opportunities. Many opportunities will come disguised. When we make it a habit to look at everything as an opportunity, we open up the possibility for growth and change. It is part of having a positive and possible outlook.

Keep your eyes open when meeting people and have the courage to look for opportunities for growth.

The world is full of business advice. Do this, don't do that. However, I have learned that it is not about a list of things to do but a mindset. If we can look at the world with a calm, practical eye that sees possibilities, we will not only see opportunity everywhere, but we will find the best way to navigate the business world and strengthen our future with community and connections.

THINK YOUR WAY TO THE TOP BUSINESS RESOURCES

PUBLICATIONS

Harvard Business Review - A highly respected and informative publication covering business strategy, management, and leadership. It is known for publishing articles that challenge conventional wisdom and provide cutting-edge insights into the business world.

Forbes - A popular business publication that covers the latest trends, news, and insights in the world of business. It is read by millions of people worldwide and is a trusted source of information for investors, entrepreneurs, and business professionals.

Inc.com - A digital magazine for entrepreneurs, small business owners, and startups, providing practical advice, news, and resources. It is a valuable resource for anyone working to grow their business, develop their leadership skills, or stay up to date on the latest industry trends.

Entrepreneur.com - An online magazine with a focus on entrepreneurship, startups, and small business. It features articles written by successful entrepreneurs, thought leaders, and business experts, making it a go-to resource for aspiring and established entrepreneurs alike.

Fast Company - A business magazine that focuses on innovation, creativity, and the future of business. Its articles explore the latest technological advancements, emerging trends, and disruptive ideas that are shaping the business world.

Business Insider - A digital news publication covering business, finance, tech, politics, and more. Its articles are known for their in-depth analysis, engaging writing style, and comprehensive coverage of breaking news and trends.

Nathan Barry's Newsletter - A weekly newsletter by Nathan Barry, the founder of ConvertKit, that shares insights on entrepreneurship, marketing, and product development. It is highly regarded for its practical advice, actionable tips, and inspiring stories of successful entrepreneurs.

BOOKS

***The Right Kind of Rich* by Ron Osborne** - My first book! An inspiring and insightful memoir that offers a unique perspective on achieving success in business and life. It is a must-read for anyone aspiring to overcome adversity and achieve their dreams.

***The Lean Startup* by Eric Ries** - A classic book on entrepreneurship that has revolutionized the way start-ups are built and launched. It is a practical guide that offers actionable advice and real-world examples for aspiring entrepreneurs.

***The Complete Leader* by Ron Price** - A comprehensive leadership guide that covers everything from self-awareness to team building. It is a valuable resource for anyone working to improve their leadership skills and build high-performing teams.

***The Four-Hour Work Week* by Tim Ferriss** - A game-changing book that challenges conventional notions of work and productivity. It offers practical advice and strategies for achieving more with less and living life on your own terms.

***Working in Sync* by Whit Mitchell** - The story of how 11 Dartmouth athletes propelled their college sports experience into professional excellence. It is a must-read for anyone who wants to improve their teamwork skills and achieve success in any field.

***The E-Myth Revisited* by Michael E. Gerber** - A classic business book that offers a step-by-step guide for building a successful business using a franchise model. It is a must-read for anyone who wants to start or grow a business.

***Good to Great* by Jim Collins** - A landmark book that explores what makes great companies great. It offers practical advice and insights for anyone working to build a successful organization and achieve long-term success.

***The Investors Guide to Growing Wealth in Self Storage* by AJ Osborne** - My son's step-by-step playbook for turning a real estate asset into a thriving self storage business. It's an invaluable resource for anyone who wants to invest in self storage real estate.

***Clockwork*, Revised and Expanded by Mike Michalowicz** - A practical guide for entrepreneurs to help them streamline their business operations and achieve more with less. It offers actionable advice and strategies for building a self-sustaining business that runs like clockwork.

PROFESSIONAL NETWORKING

LinkedIn - The world's largest professional networking site, with more than 700 million members in over 200 countries. It provides a platform for individuals to showcase their skills, connect with other professionals, and stay up to date on industry news and trends.

Indeed.com - A leading job search website that provides job seekers with access to millions of job listings from thousands of company websites and job boards. It also offers insights into companies and their hiring processes, making it a valuable resource for anyone looking for a new job or career.

ONLINE LEARNING AND TEACHING

Coursera - Partners with top universities and organizations to offer online courses and degrees in a variety of subjects. It has over 82 million registered learners and 200+ top-ranked university partners, making it a popular choice for those looking to learn new skills or further their education.

Udemy - A global marketplace for online learning that connects learners with instructors offering courses in over 65 languages. With over 155,000 courses and 70,000 instructors, it provides learners with a wide range of options to choose from and learn at their own pace.

Skillshare - A platform that allows creators to share their knowledge and teach others through video-based classes. It covers topics ranging from design, business, and technology to culinary arts, music, and writing, making it a great option for anyone interested in learning a new skill or hobby.

HubSpot Academy - A free online training platform that offers courses and certifications in inbound marketing, sales, and customer service. It also provides tools and resources for professionals who want to develop their skills and advance their careers in these areas.

Teachable - An all-in-one platform that allows creators to build and sell online courses and coaching services. It provides a variety of tools and resources to help course creators build engaging and effective courses, market them, and track their success.

Thinkific – An online course platform that allows entrepreneurs and businesses to create and sell online courses and membership sites. With its user-friendly interface and robust features, it has become a popular choice for anyone who wants to monetize their expertise and build an online course business.

DIGITAL ANALYTICS & MARKETING

Google Analytics - A free web analytics service that allows website owners to track and analyze website traffic and user behavior. It provides insights into user demographics, behavior, and preferences, helping businesses make data-driven decisions and improve website performance.

Mailchimp - An all-in-one marketing automation platform that helps businesses manage their email marketing campaigns, social media ads, landing pages, and more. It also provides analytics and insights to help businesses measure the effectiveness of their marketing efforts and make data-driven decisions.

Canva – A user-friendly graphic design platform that allows businesses and individuals to create professional-looking graphics, presentations, and visual content with ease. It provides a wide range of templates, graphics, and design tools, making it a popular choice for those who don't have graphic design expertise.

Hootsuite - A social media management platform that helps businesses manage and schedule social media content across multiple platforms, including Facebook, Twitter, Instagram, and LinkedIn. It also provides analytics and insights to help businesses track the performance of their social media campaigns and improve their social media strategy.

Moz - A search engine optimization (SEO) tool that helps businesses improve their search engine rankings and online visibility. It provides insights into website traffic, keyword rankings, and backlink profiles, allowing businesses to make data-driven decisions to improve their website's search engine ranking and increase their online visibility.

PROJECT MANAGEMENT

Slack - A messaging platform that allows teams to collaborate and communicate in real-time. Its features include customizable channels, file sharing, and integration with other tools and services.

Trello - A project management tool that allows teams to organize and track tasks and projects. Its features include customizable boards, cards, and lists, as well as collaboration and automation tools.

Asana - A project management tool that allows teams to manage projects, tasks, and deadlines. Its features include customizable dashboards, project tracking, and team communication and collaboration tools.

Zoom - A video conferencing tool that allows teams to collaborate remotely. Its features include HD video and audio, screen sharing, and virtual backgrounds.

Microsoft Teams - The hub for team collaboration in Microsoft 365. Its features include chat, video conferencing, file sharing, and integration with other Microsoft Office apps.

ACCOUNTING

QuickBooks - A cloud-based accounting software that helps small businesses manage their finances, from creating invoices and tracking expenses to generating reports and managing payroll. With features such as automatic bank syncing, mobile access, and integrations with popular apps, QuickBooks offers a comprehensive solution for financial management.

Wave Accounting - A company that provides financial services and software for small businesses, including accounting, invoicing, and payroll. With its free accounting software and affordable paid services, Wave makes it easy for small business owners to manage their finances without breaking the bank.

TravelBank - An app to help you track business and travel expenses quickly and easily, from capturing receipts to submitting expense reports. With features such as automatic expense categorization, real-time policy compliance, and built-in rewards for saving money, TravelBank helps businesses save time and money on expense management.

WRITING SKILLS

***25 Absolutely Essential Things You Need to Know About Writing and Publishing a Book* by Maryanna Young** - A comprehensive guide that offers practical tips and advice for aspiring authors who want to write and publish their first book. It covers everything from developing a writing routine to marketing and promoting your book effectively.

Hemingway App - A powerful writing tool that helps users simplify their writing style and make their text more readable. It analyzes your sentences and suggests improvements to help you write with clarity and impact.

Grammarly - A popular digital writing tool that can help writers of all levels improve their writing skills. It offers suggestions for grammar, spelling, and punctuation and can help you write more clearly and confidently in a range of contexts, from emails to academic papers.

ACKNOWLEDGMENTS

I am deeply grateful to the numerous individuals who have shaped my life and the creation of this book. Their impact is evident in the principles that have shaped me and laid the foundation for my successful businesses.

My wife, Carla, has been my unwavering support and partner in life, and I am thankful for her dedication to me, our children, and our grandchildren. I am also grateful beyond words to my four amazing children and their spouses for their unique strengths, achievements, and love. My life has also been enhanced by the unconditional love and support of my mother, in-laws, and incredible grandchildren. Each member of our family brings their distinct personalities and talents to the table. Their contributions have enriched my life in countless ways.

I am also indebted to the mentors who have guided and inspired me, providing encouragement and wisdom that have allowed me to overcome my difficult upbringing and reach a place personally and professionally that I thought were only dreams.

Lastly, I express my heartfelt appreciation to the talented team at Aloha Publishing, including Maryanna Young, Heather Goetter, and the entire team, who have worked diligently to create a captivating and meaningful book that I hope will inspire and challenge young and not-so-young readers. Their dedication to merging my story with important business and personal principles has resulted in a book that reflects the power of relationships, a business mindset, and personal growth.

ABOUT THE AUTHOR

Ron Osborne is the founder and CEO of Bitterroot Holdings and president of Cedar Creek Capital, both based in Eagle, Idaho.

Ron was born into extreme poverty. As a child, he learned the importance of relationships early and actively sought personal role models and people from whom he could learn healthy financial principles. Not wanting to be held back by the mindset of his family and local community, Ron spent years learning how to change his thoughts and actions so that he, his kids, and his grandkids could lead a different life. He wanted them to understand the possibilities that come from living a life of generosity, hard work, and freedom.

Ron worked in the insurance industry for over 30 years, both for corporations and for himself. In 1997, Ron co-founded Western Benefit Solutions, an insurance brokerage, and grew it into a successful employee benefits brokerage firm based in Idaho with clients all around the United States. He sold Western Benefit Solutions to an international insurance brokerage firm in 2012.

That same year, he dove into the self-storage business with his eldest son, AJ, and son-in-law, Sam, founding Bitterroot Holdings, which focuses almost exclusively on self-storage commercial real estate. He sold the company to an international insurance brokerage firm in 2012. That same year, he founded Bitterroot Holdings, focusing almost exclusively on self-storage commercial real estate, which he had been involved with since 2005.

Ron currently lives in Meridian, Idaho, with his beautiful wife, Carla, and eight extraordinary horses. They have four amazing adult children, two daughters-in-law, one son-in-law, and six adorable grandchildren.

www.ingramcontent.com/pod-product-compliance
Lightning Source LLC
LaVergne TN
LVHW051003080826
845145LV00009B/2433

* 9 7 8 1 6 1 2 0 6 2 9 0 7 *